A. B. Guthrie, Jr.

Fair Land, Fair Land

D1021372

HOUGHTON MIFFLIN COMPANY

BOSTON · NEW YORK

Copyright © 1982 by A. B. Guthrie, Jr.
All rights reserved

For information about permission to reproduce selections
from this book, write to Permissions, Houghton Mifflin Company,
215 Park Avenue South, New York, New York 10003.

Library of Congress Cataloging-in-Publication Data

Guthrie, A. B. (Alfred Bertram), 1901–1991
Fair land, fair land.
I. Title.
PS3513.U855F3 813'.52 82-3055
ISBN 0-395-32511-0   AACR2
ISBN 0-395-75519-0 (pbk.)

Printed in the United States of America

QUM 10 9 8 7 6 5 4 3 2 1

For information about this and other Houghton Mifflin
trade and reference books and multimedia products,
visit The Bookstore at Houghton Mifflin on the
World Wide Web at http://www.hmco.com/trade/.

To Robert F. Cubbins
my friend, promoter and goad

AUTHOR'S NOTE

I have sworn more than once to write no more about the early-day West and just as often have broken the vow. I break it again for one reason among others.

In my series of novels — mostly about the interior northwest — I left a time gap, roughly from 1845 to 1870. Here I have undertaken to fill it. Though the story is complete in itself, it belongs chronologically between *The Way West* and *These Thousand Hills*.

No writer escapes debts. My thanks then to Ruth K. Hapgood, my helpful editor; to my wife, Carol, an acute and gentle critic, and to my stepson, Bill "Herb" Luthin, no poor critic himself, both of whom have encouraged me and waited on my work almost page by page; and to the Great Falls Public Library and the Center of Military History, Department of the Army, for ready and abundant assistance.

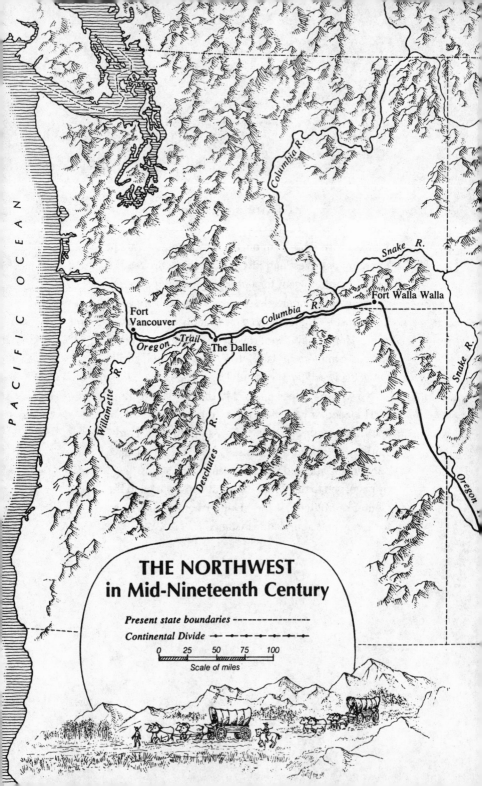

THE NORTHWEST
in Mid-Nineteenth Century

Present state boundaries - - - - - - - -
Continental Divide - - - - - - - -

0   25   50   75   100

Scale of miles

PACIFIC OCEAN

Columbia R.

Snake R.

Fort Walla Walla

Fort Vancouver

Oregon Trail

Columbia R.

The Dalles

Willamette R.

Deschutes R.

Snake R.

Oregon

Part One

Part One

1

DICK SUMMERS climbed the ridge from the channeled valley, glad enough to be leaving Oregon behind him. He hadn't said goodbye to any of the wagon-train people who had hired him for a guide. Goodbyes were something like gravestones. Yeah, rest in peace, you sod-busters. May the Lord bless you, good men and weak. Here's hoping your plows pay off in berries or melons or apples or whatever.

"Hurrah for Oregon," they had called. Sure, plant a nail and reap tomatoes. Till the soil. Put up a house. Breed chickens, pigs, sheep, cattle or whatever. Live fat right there, today, tomorrow and tomorrow. The soil, for certain, was richer than that on the stingy acres he had farmed in Missouri, but farming was still farming. Let those do it who were farm-turned.

For an instant he was back, a gray-back in Missouri, the slow sod turning to the share and the slow-poke mule farting in his face. The corn grew up spindly and the tobacco leached-looking. The hogs were growling in their pens, wanting slops.

No more of that for him. Good for them as liked it. Boresome life if not. He ought to know. He had tried it while married to a good if sickly wife who got as tiresome as the chores. He could count as fun only the careful training of a good horse.

Even high on the ridge the breath of the Pacific reached him, wet enough and salt enough to pickle pork in. Going east he was, going east to find the west, the west of wind and open skies and buffalo. Hurrah for that.

He shifted his hold on his Hawken. It was all he carried, it and his old Green River knife, some ammunition and a small sack of possibles.

He veered off to the edge of the Columbia's gorge, lay down and peered over. Far below him, almost straight below, the rushing river ran. Here was beaver country, too, though not much to his liking. Or it had been beaver country, the whole scoop of it, north, south and east, when there were plenty beaver and the price good enough to attract men and companies. Hudson's Bay men had trapped clear into California and east of there in territory claimed by Americans who weren't too careful themselves, both sides being plenty willing to poach.

He ought to be getting on, he thought, but for a moment let his mind play with the great cargoes and pack-train harvests of furs that meant fame for Fort Vancouver and money for Hudson's Bay. What would the fort do now, with beaver scarce and worth next to nothing? What would old Here Before Christ do?

He squirmed back from the cliff's edge and started walking again. Here had been beaver country all right, but give him the Popo Agie and the Wind and the Seeds-kee-dee and throw in the upper Missouri in spite of the Blackfeet. Give him a far reach of eye, the grasses rippling, the small streams talking, buttes swimming clear a hundred miles away. Give him not Mount Hood but the clean, ungodly upthrust of the Tetons. They were some.

He was hankering for the young years, for the new land and the frolics he had been part of, and he shrugged to shake the hankering out of his head. Like a tomfool he had spent too much time remembering and, remembering, had rushed toward old age, at least in his mind. He was maybe sixteen when, with a scatter of education, enough to read, write and cipher up to a point, he had quit his no-account home in Missouri. Two years later he had gone up the Platte and learned to trap beaver. No sooner was he in the settlements again than he began to hark back, as if the best part of his life was behind him. That's the way it had been. Later he had gone up the Missouri and into the country of the Roche Jaune and then again up the Platte and over South Pass to the Seeds-kee-dee and had wintered in South Park and so become a *hivernan* or sure enough mountain man. Next, up the Missouri in a keelboat, and most of the party, all except three, rubbed out by the Blackfeet. And each trip was a remembered trip, too much remembered. Afterward, feeling old, he had gone back to his farm and stayed there until the party bound for Oregon had wanted him as a guide.

He plodded on, feeling the ocean mist closing in.

How the hell old was he, anyhow? Christ maybe knew. Couldn't be much more than forty-five, if that, but the western winds wrote time in a man's face, and the sun and wind bleached what hair hadn't turned white, and anyone who had spent more than one season in the mountains was likely to get "old" attached to his name.

But that wasn't the point. The point was he kept looking back, like a grandpa returned in mind to his pup days.

He halted at a trickle of spring water and drank, belly down. Time, he thought, getting up and going on. There was no such thing as time, then, now or ever. Time was always. It was the changes, the trappings along the way, that a man reckoned his life by. Rendezvous dead and gone, along with plenty of those who had enjoyed it. Beaver nigh gone. Fur companies and some sometime mountain men making out with coarse furs. Before a man knew it the buffalo might all be killed off. Another marking, another trapping to reckon by. That was the way of men and things. Find a good country and spoil it.

Maybe only mountains lasted, like Mount Hood yonder, dimmed by the mist.

He came to a stream he didn't know the name of and shucked off his clothes and waded across with his plunder. As long as he was at it, he might as well clean himself up where he didn't have to watch for womenfolk.

Dressing, he thought he'd put on his old buckskins once he got to buffalo country. Homespun and peg boots were all right for now. He bet his feet would be tender in moccasins.

Mountains lasted and what else? The sky. The stars. Maybe the high plains and the riffling grasses, though like as not men would find a use for the land and gouge it up so's to raise turnips and cabbages or some other truck not worth eating. Before that was done, he aimed to have a long, good look again.

But even a turnip would sit all right now. He had been walking for eight hours or so by the look of the sun that was trying to show through the mist, and he hadn't brought even a bite to tide him over. No matter. A mountain man could make out.

Make out then, he told himself. Look sharp. Must be some kind of game in this teary country, small game, anyhow, but the Hawken was too large for a rabbit or bird. It would make mush of the meat.

To his right appeared a likely stand of evergreens, pines or spruces, he couldn't tell which. He walked to it, going soft, and after what seemed a long time heard little throat cluckings. In a small open space a few fool hens were pecking. He could kill one with a thrown rock, but the motion of his arm would probably flush the others, and he had best get two if he could.

He withdrew and found a dead limb and from his possible sack took a short length of buckskin. He made a sliding loop of it and tied it to the small end of the branch. By itself it would collapse, so he bound it around with long stems of green grass.

He went back to the clearing and sat down, moving slow. It

was movement and not unmoving presence that spooked critters. The birds didn't scare. They looked at him with their little snake eyes and went back to feeding. He snared one and
drew it to him, the others just watching it flutter. He broke its
neck with his fingers. He didn't need the noose for the second
one. It came close, and he reversed his pole and tapped it on
the head with the butt end.

At a ribbon of water he cleaned and plucked the birds and
went on until he came to a low bank. It would shut off the wind
if the wind blew and reflect heat from the fire if he needed it
during the night. He gathered wood, built a small fire and let
it go down mostly to coals. He speared one bird with a green
stick and positioned it over the heat.

Watching it beginning to sizzle, he thought even a big fire
would be safe in this country. There was no gumption much in
the fish-eating Indians of the coast, no spizerinctum. But feed
them on rich buffalo meat, and they might get ringy.

When the hen was done, he ate it, wishing for salt and even
bread. That showed how far he had strayed from his mountain-
man days. In time fur hunters lost their taste for both, as he
had once. He wrapped the other bird in a piece of canvas and
tied it in a tree.

He smoothed out his possible sack so's to have something to
rest his head on and lay down, the Hawken by his side. He
would drowse off, he thought, by thinking of Chief White
Hawk of the Shoshones and a squaw lying willing under a robe.

2

HE WAS DRIFTING into light sleep when a voice came out of the darkness. "Hello, the fire."

He sat up, his hand closing on his rifle. "Step ahead."

A form took shape, a long and skinny form in old buckskin. "No cause for the shootin' iron, friend."

"Come and set then." Summers tossed a couple of sticks on the dying fire.

"Wanted to make sure what was what. I got a couple of horses. Wait till I tend to them." When the man returned, he carried a jug. He sat down by the fire. "Don't know about you, but I could do with a dram."

"Sure thing."

The man was probably thirty-odd years old. His clean-shaven face had known weather. He uncorked the jug, held it out and Summers drank.

"Name's Birdwhistle. Birdy, they call me."

"I've heerd the name in the settlements. Bound west?"

"My mind goes back and forth, like a dog that keeps runnin' out to bark and keeps runnin' back, scared of what he's barkin' at." Birdwhistle took time to drink. "I went west with a party and decided I didn't like it much, so I started back by myself. A couple or three days out, and I thought, what's the idee, goin' back to what you come from?"

A couple of stars shone through the mist. The night was silent, without a bird or coyote sounding off. Birdwhistle asked, "Bound back yourself?"

"Partways, anyhow."

"Well, there I was, with two minds, so to speak. I'm a fair hand with horses and machinery and good with a hammer and saw, and I figured latelike, though I knew it damn well, that there would be plenty of work in Oregon, not like in the settlements, and, hell, I could stand rain. So I turned ass-around."

"Meet anybody?"

"There was a party herdin' cows west."

"How far away?"

"Two days, maybe a little more, from here. Why?"

"Friends of mine."

"I take it you been a mountain man?"

"How so?"

"The Hawken and the looks of you. The mountains put a brand on a man."

"Onct I was."

"Me, too. I trapped beaver and went to one rendezvous, but I was never no great shakes. That rendezvous! I come out of it with a dose of the clap and a case of bottle fever that would have made God cry. That was toward the tail end of things."

Summers said, "It all petered out."

The man was full of talk, so let him talk.

"Fun while it lasted, though. We wasn't pups, most of us, but it was like pups we played. All that crazy language. 'This child' and 'This nigger' for your own self and all those damn 'waghs.' It kind of sticks to me yet."

For the hell of it, Summers said, " 'Pears like it does to this child. That it does."

Birdwhistle chuckled. "Like you said, it all petered out. Me and some others hung on for a while, takin' few furs and tradin' them for nothin'. Then we tried that new wrinkle, hide-huntin'."

"Poor doin's."

"And poorer because of the bunch I was with. There was one man, the ringleader, scared the shit out of me." Birdwhistle drank and shook his head. "The broodiest bastard I ever see. Turn on you for nothin'. He killed two men to my knowin'."

Summers took his turn at the jug. "Some's like that."

"A bragger, too. Taken a little drunk he would tell as how he killed his friend."

"I heard tell of one case like that."

"What did he kill him for?"

"I never got the straight of it."

"This broody bastard said his best friend was slippin' it to his squaw and even birthed a child by him. That was in Blackfoot country."

Summers asked, "Blackfoot?"

"So he said. I figure he was warnin' us to lay off whatever squaw he had taken up with. Then again he would be dead quiet and grumpy, like as if he couldn't get along with hisself. Better leave him plumb alone then. Broody was what they called him, not when he was around."

"Just Broody, huh?"

"To his face we called him Boone."

Without knowing it until it was done, Summers sucked in a deep breath. "Last name Caudill?"

"Come to think on it, maybe it was. Know him?"

Know him! Know Boone Caudill? Know Jim Deakins, the friend Boone had killed. Over the few years there had been the three of them, all friends, so he had thought, partners in hardship and frolic, until he had felt too old for the life and left them before they set out for the north country. They mixed in his mind, they and what they had done, and he forgot to answer until the man asked again, "Did you?"

"Yup. I knew him."

"Beggin' your pardon, but can I ask the name that you go by?"

"Dick Summers."

The man whistled a low whistle. "Dick Summers!" He held out his hand for a shake. "Never expected to meet up with you."

"Where were they when you last heard?"

"Broody and that bunch? Tradin' at Bent's Fort, but that was a time ago. You aim to find them?"

"Might run into them. Who knows?"

"Watch out for that Broody."

"Yeah."

Birdwhistle sat silent. A little flare of the fire deepened his wrinkles. At last he said, "Someone's bound to kill him, but it won't be me."

"Yeah."

"Killin' his friend over a squaw for God's sake!"

"And the friend never done him wrong."

"How you know?"

"I knew the friend."

"Beggin' your pardon again, but you got a grudge?"

"I don't know as killin' a man ever sets things right."

The man took a long look at him and said at the end of it, "I wouldn't want to be Broody."

3

CURTIS MACK sat on a downed log and smoked his first pipe of the day. He was tired, as everyone else was, and ought to be up helping pitch camp, but for a moment damned if he wouldn't just sit and puff.

It was raining again, if that was news, raining a mist with few real drops in it. Low in the west the sun was drowning, yet an hour or so of daylight remained. Tomorrow they'd take the day off, he and the single men who were trailing livestock overland from the Dalles to the Willamette where the Oregon party would claim them. A day off was justified, for here they were without the loss of a single animal and the hardest going was surely behind them. An insane thing, to volunteer to lead the crew, but by God he was doing it.

Higgins was undoing the packs and taking out cooking utensils and food. The pack animals, rid of their burdens, had rolled and gone to drink and were mingling with the other stock, loosely herded by the men on horseback. The men had little to worry about. On this upland clearing was water, good feed and soft turf for sore feet. The riders called out now and then, more to relieve tedium than to discourage bunch-quitters. Their voices sounded tired and wet.

By and by he and Higgins would put up a fly so the men could sleep more or less dry, and there was the fire to make and the meal to be heated. Meal? Salmon and rice again and coffee that had lost its flavor. With what good nature they could summon, the men complained of this steady and indifferent fare. Tobacco was short-rationed, too. The wonder was that the crew wasn't really grumpy.

Higgins stepped toward him and asked, "Hey, you hear a shot?"

"Don't think so."

"Maybe it was just in my mind. No game in this whole scoop of country, far as we've seen."

"Nothing to be alarmed about at any rate."

Higgins shook his head, as if to rid it of imagined sound, but still said, "I swear it didn't sound much more'n a whoop and a holler away."

"Anyhow, we'd better put the fly up and then start a fire."

"Yeah."

They strung a rope between two trees at the edge of the clearing, threw the canvas over it and spread and secured the sides, tying them to what growth was handy.

Higgins said, "Now I'll gather the makin's of a fire, if so we can light this damn wet wood."

"No big hurry. The stock hasn't bedded down yet."

Higgins sat on the log beside him, saying, "I don't know about Oregon. It's so goddamn rainy. Here we are, all of us, smellin' like wet dogs."

"Wait till we get there. It's too early for judgments."

"Maybe so, but first acquaintance ain't promisin'."

One of the riders called out, and Higgins got up and squinted. "There's a man afoot on the way."

"I can see him."

"Got a rifle. Walks like an Injun. Look! Botter and Moss wavin' him welcome. Damn my soul if it ain't Dick Summers!"

"It can't be, but still — "

It did turn out to be Summers. He came into camp smiling, asking, "How be ye?" He shook the offered hands.

"You don't bring bad news?" Mack asked, suddenly fearful.

"Naw. Naw. All fat and sassy."

"My wife?"

"Same with her. I left the bunch on safe water, making for the Willamette. Could be they're stakin' claims by now, though it's a mite soon."

The men on horseback had ridden close, casting their eyes back now and then to make sure the herd was safe. It was. Through the gathering dark Mack could make out that some of the animals were lying down.

Mack motioned toward the log he'd been sitting on and said, "Rest yourself."

Before Mack could speak, Higgins asked the question. "How come you're here, Dick?"

Summers smiled and answered, "They showed me a plow, and I took off." His eyes moved from the men to the resting livestock to the camp, and Mack thought he knew what Summers had noted. He said, "I had to leave the wagons behind. My mistake, I suppose. I heard a man named Barstow was building a wagon road, but it runs south of here, and I counted on a shortcut."

"Worst part's behind you, I'm thinkin'."

Higgins put in, "Leastwise, we didn't have to shed any plunder."

"Thanks to you," Mack answered. Then to Summers, "He made pack saddles out of some lumber we had. And it was his idea to lash poles to the sides of the oxen, make rope platforms behind, load the stuff on and let the poles drag."

"All the same Indians," Summers said. "Travois."

Mack relighted his pipe. "What the Oregon party was shy of — what we're shy of — is what we should have given thought to. Horseshoes, for heaven's sake. Hig has his tools but no forge of course, and he has to do what fitting he can with what few shoes we have." He flung out a hand, feeling the oversight, himself guilty as any, feeling sore-footed himself. "Sand, water and rock, what they do to hooves! Painful to watch, I tell you."

Summers nodded. "Oxen get sore-footed, too, as you've seen for yourself, but I don't put stock in ox shoes. For not havin' enough horseshoes, I fault myself some, but that don't help. For any sore-footed critter the only answer is rest on soft turf."

"We're resting tomorrow," Mack said.

"Rest and trimmin', which Hig can do." Summers fell silent, then his gaze went to Higgins. "You reckon you could make a couple of pack saddles for me?"

"I come high."

"Higher'n fresh meat, old hoss?"

Higgins smiled his toothless smile. Looking at him for an instant, Mack thought how poor a specimen he appeared. Broken mouth, pinched-up face, thin and gangly frame. Yet he was the best member of the crew.

"You might think I can't chaw," Higgins answered, "but I got some grinders in back, up and down both, and they team up good. My mouth's waterin', but time you brought us fresh meat, I could build enough saddles for the cavalry."

"Hey, wait, Hig," Mack said. "You said you heard a shot?"

"Thought I did."

"How about it, Summers?"

"Could have. Up the line a ways a cow elk stepped out — only real meat in Oregon, I reckon — and stood waitin' for me to shoot, and, hearin' your men callin' like with empty bellies,

I obliged. The carcass ain't so far, all gutted out, ready to cut up and load."

One of the riders said, "Goodbye to that goddamn salmon," and another followed with, "I just changed my mind. Never before now did I think the Lord would provide."

"Botter, Insko," Mack called out. "Catch up a couple of pack horses and fetch that meat." He turned to Summers. "Can they find it?"

Summers said to the men, "Stick close to the bank. The critter's out in the open. I got it flagged."

While Botter and Insko rode out to catch pack horses and Moss went to keep watch on the stock, Mack said, "Looks like you're the answer to prayer, Dick."

"Thank the elk. Me, I been livin' on wild chicken. Any more of them, and I'll grow feathers or lay an egg."

"Now to get a good fire going," Mack said.

"A miracle you want now," Higgins answered. "Wood wet as water but not much wetter'n me. Rain's let up anyhow. You got ideas about a fire, Dick?"

"I've built some."

"Want to build another?"

"What you been burnin'?"

Mack answered, "What we can drag in. Downed stuff. Dead fall. What else?"

Summers was silent.

"I suppose you know something better?" Mack hadn't meant to let the edge of irritation get into his voice.

Summers gave him his smile. "You can make out all right. Done it so far."

"Looky here, Dick," Higgins said. "Don't get shit in your gizzard. We're askin', friendly." Not for the first time Mack felt grateful to Higgins. The man had a habit of seeing and setting things straight.

"Was it me," Summers said then, "I'm thinkin' I would knock off the low-growin' branches from pine trees. Most of 'em's dead. Most of 'em's dry, bein' sheltered by them growin' above."

Mack looked up at the great trees that rose around the camp. The first branches were far beyond reach, sprouting out fifty or more feet over their heads. "Good idea," he said, "if we had some trained monkeys."

Higgins picked up an ax. "I know where some runt stuff is at. Red meat deserves a good fire, not like sour salmon."

While he was gone, Summers asked, "You got an old piece of wipe rag — it don't need to be big — and some grease?"

"Rags, sure, but grease?"

"Nice bacon fat," Summers said, grinning.

"Last I saw of it was far down on the Platte. But, hey, what about axle grease? I don't know why we brought it along. No dry axles since we left the wagons."

"Might do. Won't hurt to try."

Mack went to the packs and returned with a strip of cloth and a bucket.

Summers spread grease on the rag, sprinkled powder from his horn on the grease and worked it in.

"Do you always go to such pains?" Mack asked.

"Nope. It's just you wanted a good fire quick for them steaks."

Higgins came back with an armload of branches. Summers took one of them, got out his knife and began cutting shavings, thin as ribbons. Nothing but a razor-sharp blade could do that, and Mack wondered how the man kept his knife in such shape.

Summers put the shavings over the rag, added some fine twigs, poured a bit of gunpowder under one end of the rag and withdrew flint and steel from his possible sack. He rubbed the powder from his hands on his pants legs and then struck a spark. The bit of powder went up in a puff but still ignited the rag. As the fire spread sputtering along it, lighting the shavings, Higgins said, "By God, a slow fuse."

It was dark now and clear of mist. Higgins built up the fire and started heating frying pans. The night was quiet except for the crackling of the fire and now and then a sneeze from one of the loose horses. Then came the sound of hooves and the creaking of gear.

Botter and Insko slipped from their saddles and were quick to unload the pack horses. Unloading, Botter said, "I found the heart with the guts, all mangled to hell and not fit to eat. A thinkin' man wouldn't have ruint the heart."

"Yeah, Botter," Insko answered. "Was it you, you'd have shot the elk in the asshole so's not to break the skin. On'y you'd never have spotted game in the first place."

It was good, their joking was, Mack thought. The promise of a mere change of diet lifted all spirits. Small as it was on any big scale, why shouldn't it? Men lived more by little things than big.

Botter was knifing and peeling the hide from a hind quarter. "Keep your goddamn distance, Insko," he said. "You'll taint the meat."

"It's beyond taintin' with you workin' on it."

Higgins took a fresh-cut steak and plopped it in a hot pan. Then he passed out tin plates, knives and forks.

Mack had seen hungry men eat, but never, he thought, had he seen appetites like these. One steak followed another onto plates and into mouths, and still the men looked hungrily at the frying pans.

"One of you feel like relieving Moss?" he asked finally.

Insko got up, saying, "He's probably fell off his horse, smellin' the meat. I'll go see, but keep the irons hot."

In his bedroll under the fly that night, only now and then hearing the soft tone of a bell he had strapped on one of the horses, Mack thought about Summers, Summers with his easy smile and gray eyes and all-around competence. Without being pushy, he was too damn good, that man, and here he was about to set out for God knew where. What ate at him? What shoved him? Many a man would have settled for what Summers was. That, he thought, again with the edge of envy, included himself.

4

MACK LEFT THE LOOSE STOCK just as dawn was breaking. To Botter, who was relieving him, he said, "They hardly need watching." He had taken the early-morning shift, the one the men disliked most, and even his presence hadn't been necessary. The sore-footed animals had stayed put. For all the roaming they did, they might have been under fence.

The day gave promise of being clear for a change. Any foresighted man, looking at the forest around the clearing, would have seen opportunity, he thought. Some of the trees were as big as tulip poplars, just one of which would and had supplied enough lumber for a two-story house and a good barn. Settlements and settlers needed wood. They needed planks, studs, shingles and all manner of milled stuff. And here for the cutting and there for the cutting were these conifers — pine, spruce and fir, he guessed — and down toward the river bottoms were other great trees, their leafage frondlike, which someone had supposed were western cedar. He had the capital for a start. He would go into the lumber business and grow with it. He was arriving at the right time.

You took Oregon or you left it. Rain or not, he would take. He could see himself supplying lumber for great cities, for a thousand towns, for farms to be.

Riding through lush and strange vegetation, he could see the campfire winking. Summers' work probably, or maybe Higgins'. A good sight, and he breathed deep. Mount Hood rose yonder, as big as ambition.

Insko and Moss were coming out from under the fly and making for the little stream to wash up. It was a good guess that they would have slept longer but for the thought of red meat.

"Seems like a nice, lazy day," Higgins said to him as he climbed from his horse.

"I think we've earned it." Mack let the horse loose. It wouldn't go far with the reins trailing. The eastern sky flushed before the upcoming sun.

"Put some meat on for you?"

"Wait till I wash."

He came back to the fire, following Insko and Moss and told Higgins, "Slap it on."

"Want some flapjacks to go with it?"

"God, no." Having nothing better, Higgins had been making pancakes with weevily flour, water and saleratus.

"Not for me, neither," Moss said, and Insko came on with, "Same here."

The men ate hugely again, and presently Moss said, wiping his mouth with the back of his hand, "I'll go spell Botter long enough for him to feed his face."

Beyond a bare word or two Summers had been silent. After he had chewed the last bite on his plate, he said, "Meat's meat, come to that, but I swear I've tasted better."

"Not me," Insko answered. "What's better?"

"Buffler for one, and I've set my teeth into some good mountain sheep. I've knowed men said painter meat was best of all."

"Cat meat!" Mack said. "God save me."

"Meat's meat, like I said."

Botter came in and had his meal, and all hands, except one herder, lazed around afterward, no one seeming to be in a hurry. Summers sat on the ground, his knees folded in front of him. Higgins tried the same position but shortly gave up and took a seat on the log that Mack occupied. Botter rode out to resume his watch. Insko disappeared into the trees, presumably to relieve himself.

"Dick," Mack said, "you haven't told us where you were going?"

"Maybe I ain't sure myself."

"Back over the trail, I bet, back over South Pass if the weather lets you."

"I'm not plannin' on it."

"Then where?"

"Just kind of follow my nose." Summers made a backward movement with his thumb. "Lots of places that way but no place in particular. Just yonder."

Higgins broke in. "You tempt a man, Summers."

Mack turned on him. "Don't talk crazy, Hig. You want to get to the Willamette. You want to get there."

Higgins chewed on a stem of grass, his crowded eyes thoughtful. "The trouble with there is there," he said and paused.

"That's quite a cryptic remark, wouldn't you say?"

"My maw never taught me them big words, and about all my old man taught me was how to shoot squirrels and drink out of a jug. Most of what I know I learned fixin' things, that and workin' in a blacksmith shop."

"That explains things, I suppose?"

"I come over the trail with Mr. Fairman, eatin' his grub and workin' it out in trade. I mean helpin' him with whatever I could. He don't need me now. Neither do you for a fact."

"I wouldn't quite say that."

"Just too polite, you are."

With a stick Summers was making idle lines on the ground.

"Anyhow, let's get down to it, Hig," Mack went on. "I don't understand. What is it that really tempts you? What's the trouble with there?"

"There? Well, I figure this way. There is there all right, until a man gets to it. Then it ain't there. It's here, and here is what you wanted to get away from in the first place."

Mack shook his head. "The only way out that I can see for you is for you to shoot yourself."

"Not as long as there's trails I never took. Not while there be yonders and yonders. Ain't I right, Dick?"

Summers looked up. His gray eyes glinted. "That's a way of lookin' at it."

Mack said, "You're a great josher, Hig. Now come off it. I know you can't be serious."

"That depends. I got two horses that Mr. Fairman gave me." Higgins turned to face Summers. "Not meanin' to shove myself in and beggin' your pardon, but would you keer to two it?"

"Still got your fiddle?"

"Sure thing."

"Sometimes I hanker for music."

The deal was made then, Mack knew. Two wild men, bound into the nowheres of wilderness. For a flash he wished he were one of them, footloose, worry-free, rid of ambition, following his nose into the yonders of the world.

The wish left him as quickly as it had come. What a way to live! Always poor in pocket. Never settled. Enduring the pinched, mean life of camp after camp, with camp smoke in their eyes and the cold biting at them. Wilderness bums, womanless, childless, without goals.

That was their future. It was if they beat or survived the

snows of winter, if they made it over the high, bitter passes and came out on the plains. Already the season was advanced.

"Time to pack up, I reckon," Summers said, rising. "I got two horses in the bunch."

"I'll tack some horseshoes on if I can find any that come close to a fit," Higgins said.

"If anyone can catch that spooky horse of Dick's." Mack doubted that anyone could.

"You mean my Feather?"

"Feather in a high wind is more like it."

"Reckon I should have told you. He's whip-broke."

"Whatever that means."

"Closer to the mark to say plank-broke." Summers was looking toward the horses. They were grazing near, Feather in the forefront as usual, his bay coat shining.

"I had him since he was a colt," Summers went on. "You know how it is. Get a horse in a corral, and, not likin' the idea of a rope or a bridle, he turns his hind end to you, even if he's pretty well broke."

"So far so good," Mack said.

"Now every time that colt did it to me, I slapped him smart with a board. Pretty soon he learned if he faced me he didn't get a lick on the ass."

"He's not in a corral now."

"No, but I drilled it into him. Horses ain't so smart in some ways. He got it into his head that wherever he was he didn't dast turn his butt to me. I'll go get him."

Summers took a piece of rope and a length of firewood and moved toward the horses. "Here, you, Feather," he called out. "Whoa now, boy."

The horse half-turned as if to run, and Summers raised the stick. "None of that now."

The horse moved to face him, its nostrils quivering. Summers slid the rope around its neck and started to lead the animal in.

"That damn man could do anything he set his mind to," Mack

said to Higgins, knowing his tone was vexed. "He's at home in the world, or could be."

"Yeah," Higgins answered as if only half-agreeing. "His world."

"And yours?"

5

THEY DIDN'T SET OUT, he and Hig, until early the next morning, Hig having said it would be a good idea to shoe all four horses, poor as the shoes might fit. That was a good idea for a fact, and he had helped while Hig tacked the shoes on and pared down the broken and flattened edges of hooves.

They rode off, Summers in the lead with one pack horse and Higgins behind with another. They signaled goodbye to the Oregon crew, itself about to mount up.

Summers was content to poke along. The morning with chilly but clear, and soon enough the sun would get busy. Why hurry? Sure, the snow might catch them, though he had a doubt about it. If it did, they could make out. Mountain men had known their lean-belly times, but how many of them had gone under?

They had found things to eat, even rattlesnakes, and had fought off the cold one way or another. He had himself.

Soon enough, he thought, they would be over the mountains and into chinook country where the long wind blew warm and chased off the frost. How to get over the mountains was the question, but he wouldn't worry his mind about that. Look for notches in the hills. Follow game trails as the Indians did, making the trails all the plainer. Unknown and trackless wilderness, hell. There were plenty of tracks if a man looked for them, if he had the good sense to follow.

At noon they got off their horses where a spring made a trickle, let the horses drink and then drank themselves. "That cold water leaves somethin' to be desired," Hig said, rubbing his belly.

"Should have brought along stuff for a picnic," Summers answered. "Only what? Brace up, Hig. We got red meat for tonight."

They had. They had taken a joint from the elk.

"Thinkin' about it just makes me ganter. But don't worry. I'm only a shadder at best."

The trail meandered, leading from bare ground into trees and back to bare ground. Where the trees grew thickest, Hig pointed to one side, calling out first, "There's where we left the wagons."

Summers reined toward the point. The wagons had been put where no chance traveler was likely to see them. The tongues were lashed up so's to keep the ends off the ground. The wheels were chalked.

"Tidy job," Summers said.

"Mack seen to that."

"Good man, Mack is."

"Right. But goddamn sober-sided. We wouldn't have got this far, though, but for him."

They moved on.

The sun was warm now, and the sky clear, though he had to look up to see it on account of the trees. Not like the plains where the eye could look at the far edges of the world, where distance danced on the slopes of buttes that might live just in the mind, where wild grasses waved in the wind. Mountains were all right unless they shouldered a man. Trees were all right unless they crowded him.

At early dusk they made camp where water was. Summers put rope hobbles on Feather, knowing if any of the horses tried to backtrack Feather would lead them. For good measure he hung a bell around Feather's neck.

He built a fire then, while Higgins chunked up the meat and threw it in a pot half-filled with water.

"Them steaks got pretty dry," he explained. "Hope you don't mind a stew? I sneaked away with some salt."

"Nope," Summers answered. "Takes longer, though."

"What have we got but time?"

Sure. They had time, all the time that was granted them, which no man could tally ahead. So take it easy. Quit fretting.

One day he would meet up with Boone Caudill, who had been his friend. What then? Something. Nothing. What the hell? At least he didn't have to worry about money, success and how the crop grew. Just watch the pot.

Higgins put the pot on the fire and sat down. He was trying to get used to a seat on the ground, Summers knew. "We goin' to climb up into the Blue Mountains, Dick?"

"Don't figure on it. At the Blues we leave the Oregon Trail, bound north of it."

"Then where?"

"Over the Bitter Roots, over the Rockies and so to the plains."

"Way I've heerd it, that would put us in Blackfoot country."

"Yup."

"Whatever you say," Higgins said. He stirred the pot with a stick. "I got it in my head you're fightin' shy of people. Ain't it so?"

"For now, anyhow."

"You got somethin' against 'em?"

"Just get tired of 'em in time. They spoil things."

"Like what?"

"Like ways of livin'. Look. The Indians had fixed things pretty nice. They killed just what they had to. They didn't count up what they had unless it was stole horses, which all of them stole when they could. They didn't have any idea of markin' off a piece of ground and sayin', 'This is mine.' The land belonged to all of 'em."

"Yeah?"

"Then along came the white man. He wanted furs. He wanted land. And for trade he brought along whiskey or what passed for it."

"I guess you couldn't blame him, except for the firewater."

The pot was beginning to boil.

"It's a way of things, and I was some part of it, trappin' beavers, findin' trails for others to follow, havin' one hell of a time without thinkin'."

Summers went silent, not knowing how to go on, feeling guilt in him. Higgins got up and poked at the fire, putting some fresh wood on.

"That don't argue that you got much against people," Higgins said.

"No. It's natural. What gets me is there's so many white people, more and more all the time. And the more there are, the pushier they get."

"You ain't goin' to change that, long as fuckin's so popular."

"I got nothin' against it."

"Me, neither, but it's what it leads to, what comes after. That's what you're sayin'."

"I reckon so."

They fell silent. Summers was just as glad to let the matter lie there. He wasn't good at explaining things, even to himself, he thought. It was the goodbyes that ate at him, the goodbyes to what was, the coming goodbyes to even what now was.

They ate before the stew was tender, gobbling it down nonetheless, and sat down by what was left of the fire.

By and by Higgins asked, "Dick, you been around. None of my business, but did you leave any young'ns around?"

"Not to my knowin'."

"I sired me a woods colt once, but it died bein' born. I wanted to marry that girl. I did for a fact. But she took up with a circuit-ridin' preacher. Pleased my maw all to hell. Out of sin into the arms of the Lord. That's what she said, not knowin' that the preacher was a bed-pounder, too."

"A heap of 'em are."

"Like you maybe made out, my maw was hell on religion. That's how come I got my first name."

"I never heerd it."

"I never tolt you, but, by God, if it ain't Hezekiah."

Summers had to laugh. "Hezekiah Higgins. Takes some breath to say."

"Now just forget it, huh?"

"Sure, Hig."

Looking up, Summers could see stars, but not at the sides, at the sides only tall trees, the trees boxing him in. Not too long, though. Not forever. "Hig," he said, "you feel like playin' your fiddle a little?"

"Sure thing."

Higgins went to a pack and got it and the bow out. He had to tune up and rosin the bow before playing.

"No jiggety stuff, please, Hig, and no holler music. Just somethin' easy."

With the fiddle under his chin Higgins said, "Call me crazy, Dick, but I make up songs for myself. Ridin' along I thought up one that fits you and maybe me, too. Want to hear it?"

"Play away."

The country's my mistress.
Why need me a wife?
My country's my mistress.
I lead a free life.

The music waved to the edge of silence. Out of Hig's broken mouth came a voice that was clean and pure and fetching.

> No one to nag me.
> I just go along.
> No one to nag me
> So join me in song.
> O-do-lee, o-do-lay, o-do-lee, o-do-lay.
> My country's my mistress.
> Why need me a wife?

6

IT WAS THE EDGE of dusk when they rode down to the smoother water of the Dalles and the Deschutes River. Where all had been bustle and worry and wagons just a spell ago, there were now only a few cast-off wagons, some past repair, and the odds-and-ends leavings of travelers bound down the river. There were, to boot, a canoe and a couple of rowboats, one water-logged, on the river's lip and a couple of cabins on the bank.

It beat hell, Higgins thought, how things could change, how folks could come and go, leaving behind them as junk what they had prized once, like a cherry chest there was no cargo space for, like a rusted anvil not worth more sweat. And where were the horses and cattle that the owners had worried about?

One cabin looked empty and deserted, but the other might

have something in it besides mice. It had a hitch rack in front of it and a slab lean-to at one side. They tied up.

"My butt's bounced enough for one day," Higgins said, getting off his horse. He had to hang on to the saddle horn for a minute to ease his legs.

"We'll see what's inside," Summers answered. "A drink would go good." But for an instant he stood there, considering. "Seems to me these cabins was just going up when we took off."

"I didn't take notice."

The door opened before they reached it, and a voice said, "Welcome, y'all." Dark as it was getting to be, Higgins could still see a chesty man, half bald, who wore an unbuttoned town vest. He showed them in, saying, "Best hold up until I can make some light." His shape moved to a mud-and-stick fireplace where a fire flickered. He put a twig in it until it caught and then lighted the wicks of a couple of oil lamps without chimneys.

"Now move up, gents. Place ain't too tidy, you can see. I was just fixin' to neat up when you showed."

As Higgins' eyes adjusted, he saw that the cabin had been divided. In the half they entered there was a bar made out of half a log with three stools in front of it. The floor was dirt.

"Stand up or sit down, whichever pleases you," the man said. "Nice day today. Faired off good. But I look for it to rain tomorrow. Somethin' tells me it's fixin' to."

"First time I've heerd your kind of talk in a coon's age," Higgins said, meaning to be pleasant. "Southern mountains, ain't it? That where you hail from?"

The man stiffened and gave him a long look. "What business is it of yours?"

"Can't a man ask a question?"

The man pushed up against the bar, his face set. "Makin' fun, huh? I'll tell you no one puts Joe Newton down."

Higgins cussed himself. He knew as well as anybody that mountaineers took offense when no offense was meant, they were so goddamn face-proud.

Before he could reply, Summers said, "Mister, we don't care shit where you're from or how you palaver. That don't matter one good goddamn. You got any whiskey? Just tell me that."

Summers hadn't raised his voice, but there was a tone in it that set the man back. So did his eyes.

The man said, "It's just, well, I got my pride."

"Good for you. My pardner was just tryin' to be friendly. No cause to get your dander up."

"All right. I got whiskey. Comes high, so I warn you."

Summers put a gold piece on the bar. It came, Higgins knew, from his pay as a guide. No greenbacks. Just honest coin.

Newton reached behind him and got two mugs and a jug. "This is s'posed to come from Kentucky, but you never know. It's prime stuff, I swear." He poured good measure. It was then he took note of the gold piece. He looked at it, hefted it. "Jesus Christopher," he said, "you expect me to make change for that?"

"Could be you got some fixin's we want."

"Could be. Like what?"

"No business talk till the liquor says yes."

"Sure. Take your time."

Higgins could feel the warmth of the whiskey in his belly. He wasn't much of a drammer, but once in a while a drink went good. He drained his glass.

"Fill 'em up again," Summers said. "Have one yourself."

"That's kindly," Newton said and reached for the jug and another glass.

Higgins thought he could speak again without roiling the man. "None of my business, but I'm askin' myself how you make out. For grub, I mean. Meat."

Newton took a swallow of whiskey and licked his lips. "That's a fair question, and I'll tell you it's not as hard as a man might think. Fish, for instance."

"Salmon, huh?"

"Durin' the run. But a man gets mighty tired of salmon."

"Strike up the band. I'll beat the big drum."

"Amen. I put out set lines for sturgeon. Some of them are Christly big and break my lines. I got one down in brine now that must have weighed nigh onto sixty pounds. Makes a nice change."

"All the same, it's not red meat."

"You'd be surprised, now all them pilgrims have left. Once in a while now a mule deer — I call 'em jackass deer on account of the ears — it kind of strolls by. I killed me one yesterday. Reminds me. You men crave some good eats?"

"I'm thinkin' so," Summers answered. "Pour another, friend, your own self included."

Before he took hold of the jug, the man added, "I can give you some good stuff, right off the loin. My woman — she's a Cayuse — pounds chokecherries fine, pits and all, and throws in some seasonin', like wild sage, I guess, and makes a sauce that I call mighty fine."

Touchy or not, Newton was from the Appalachian country, Higgins knew. The words he used and the nosy twang gave him away. Not that it made any difference.

"Might be you'll have company," Newton went on. "That is if you don't object to some warwhoop."

"Long as he don't hanker for scalps," Summers told him.

"Nothin' like that. He's kind of a preacher, I reckon, missionary-like. But his religion ain't wore so sore that he won't take a drink."

"Preachers I know like a dram so's to put more hell in their warnin's," Higgins said.

"He's half French to my notion. You know how those Frenchies are, always makin' up to squaws." He grinned suddenly, maybe thinking of himself. "Not that most don't."

"Comin' today, huh?" Higgins said, just to make talk.

"Said he would. Been gone two weeks now."

"So what you got in the tradin' line?" Summers asked. "A good rifle, maybe?"

"Not like that there cannon of yours. Hawken, ain't it? But I got a good Kentucky, full stock, sugar wood. Big enough for deer, even elk. It shoots true."

"Might have a look later. How's the jug holdin' up?"

Newton renewed the drinks. "Got here too late for rich pickin's," he said, resting an elbow on the bar. "Started the cabin and then figured what the hell. No goods to sell. I contracted for two wagonsful, and they was long comin'. I'll do me better next season."

"Bound to be a crowd, I'm thinkin'," Summers said.

"Bein' green," Newton went on, "I stocked a heap of the wrong things. Powder and ball for one. What did a passel of farmers want with that in peaceable country? Heavy clothes for another. Should have stocked slickers. Live and learn, they say, and I'm learnin'."

"Yeah. I reckon you might as well tell your woman to be makin' that tasty sauce."

Newton disappeared through a door, and they heard him giving directions. When he came back, he asked, "Would it be fittin' to ask where you're bound?"

"East," Summers said and didn't add to it.

"Well, good luck. I sure hope you make it. It's comin' on to the second half of August, you taken note?"

"We'll make it."

Newton didn't hear him, for he was saying as the outer door opened, "How there, stranger? We been talkin' about you."

The man who entered was short, swarthy and dressed in buckskins. He wore his hair in braids. He answered, *"Comment portez-vous?"*

"Cut out the Frenchy act," Newton said. Then to Higgins and Summers, "He means how are you?"

The man took a seat, and Summers told Newton, "I'll buy a round."

Before he drank the man said, *"Merci.* I be Christian."

"I be Dick. Here's to you, Chris."

The man sipped at his whiskey, put the mug down and

answered, "No. No. My name it is Antoine. Christian my medicine."

"My mistake." Summers gestured with his left hand. "Whitman Mission?"

Again the man shook his head. "Not so. True faith for me. Book of Heaven. The big medicine."

For an instant Summers looked puzzled, but only for an instant. "The black robes?"

"*Oui. Oui,*" Antoine answered, his smile pleased. "On Racine Amère."

"He means Bitter Root country," Summers said to Higgins. "That's over the mountains." He turned back to Antoine. "You're a long way from home."

Antoine nodded. "See my friends. What you call the Umatilla, the Nez Perce, even Cayuse. Ask them come see the black robes. Find out truth."

"I take it you're a Flathead."

"White man's talk. We no flatten heads."

"Heap sorry," Summers answered. "When you go home?"

"Moon of wild rose, maybe. Many to see."

"I'm headin' that way myself."

"Ah, to see black robes?"

"Find out the truth," Summers answered, not smiling. "Not sure how to go. Think so, but not sure. You tell me?"

"*Oui. Oui.* Say you saw Antoine, yes?"

"Sure. Sure."

Summers turned his head toward Newton. "Would you ask your woman to please put another name in the pot?"

"Figured he'd be here. On you?"

"On me."

Summers and Antoine began talking sign language. It made no sense to Higgins, that waving and pointing and playing with their fingers. He paid them little mind until Summers said, "Hig, get one of them lamps, will you?"

At Summers' signal Higgins put the lamp on the floor. Summers and Antoine squatted there, and Antoine began drawing lines in the dust, explaining with more sign language.

In between gestures Summers called to Newton, "We could stand another dose of that good whiskey."

"On the house this time," Newton told him.

Higgins didn't want another drink. He was liquored up plenty as it was. He put one hand over his mug, to be told by Newton, "When Joe Newton buys, everybody drinks." The damn man was still touchy. Higgins removed his hand.

Summers and Antoine talked some more, by tongue and hand. By and by Newton said, "You boys want to neaten up, I put a bucket of water and a basin and towel out on the bench. Grub's about ready."

Higgins hadn't even seen him go out.

Antoine was the first to go wash. While he was gone, Summers told Higgins, "I figured my nose was pointed right, but now I sure God know how to go."

"Just so it gets us to yonder."

7

To Higgins, looking backward, it seemed the days and nights were all one, each different in the doing and seeing but still, taken together, all the same. Get up before the sun, eat, pack up and saddle up and ride, make camp just before dark, eat again, gab a while, sleep. And ford the rivers, the Deschutes, the John Day, the Umatilla, and maybe take time to wash the dirt off.

The trail, so far as they followed it, was empty of travelers. The Oregon-bound had passed this way, the men, the women, the children, the wagons and livestock, and had pushed on by water or trail to the promised land that he and Summers were putting behind them.

They had met some Indians along the Umatilla, a tatter-assed, beggarly bunch to whom Summers paid little attention except to call back, "Watch your outfit, Hig. They got quick hands."

The days and nights were the same but the country changed, from forest and ferns to pieces of prairie and cottonwood patches. It was good to take note of them all but bad not to know what was seen. What's the name of this plant? What kind of tree's that? A damn shame that a man went through life ignorant of the life around him. Too late, though, to do anything about that.

At the edge of the Blue Mountains Summers slanted them to the left, to the northeast. He pulled up where water ran from a spring and let the horses drink. He pointed. "Whitman Mission's over there a piece, and, I hear, a fort. Can't see 'em from here."

"You aim to skip both?"

"Palaver would just hold us up. Besides, we got what we need."

True enough, Higgins thought, though they'd have to find game for the pot. The list of things bought at the Dalles ran through his head. Two blankets to add to their bedrolls. A couple of plugs of cheap tobacco. One jug of whiskey. A square of canvas big enough for a tent. Powder and ball. A packet of salt. And for Higgins himself Summers bought a short heavy coat like his own. He called it a capote. He added warm wool pants and the Kentucky rifle. For good measure the man had thrown in a piece of salted deer meat and, at Higgins' hint, some corn meal and a trifle of honey. That wasn't all. "In them old felts you men will freeze your goddamn ears off," the man had said. "Now I got just the right thing. Can't sell 'em to sod-lovers, not in rainy country, so I'm makin' a gift." He poked through a pile of goods and came out with two coonskin caps. And he wasn't from Kentucky or Tennessee, huh?

As they were about to leave the Dalles, Higgins had said to Summers, "Dick, how in hell am I going to pay you back? You spend money like you got no use for it."

"Used it, didn't I? And where we're goin' it don't count for much. As for payin' me back, I'll worry about that when my taxes come due."

That meant never, of course, and all Higgins could think to say was, "Well, shit. Thanks."

So there, day by day, was Summers riding ahead, pushing his horse to a good clip. If he ever got tired, he didn't show it. The damn man was made of whang leather. At the end of the day he'd say, "Best just set a spell, Hig. You look fagged. I'll tend to things."

But a man couldn't let him do that, not if he had any pride, not when he must be twenty years younger.

Sometimes Higgins wondered why he trailed along. Sure, to get yonder. To see things not seen before. Just to mosey along, careless, and think free and easy. To be away from folks and close to God if there was one. All the same, he wouldn't be where he was but for the man that Summers was.

They lived on meat, deer meat mostly. It was Summers who shot it. He could see game where there couldn't be any. A time or two they ate rabbit or fool hen that Higgins bagged with his old scattergun. They were easy targets even if a man aimed at the head so's not to get birdshot in the carcass.

One morning Higgins mixed corn meal with melted meat fat, added a dab of honey, poured in hot water and made what his maw called corn dodger. Eating it, Summers smiled and said, "Please to pass the butter and buttermilk."

That was the morning Summers heated water, took from his possible sack a hunk of homemade soap brown as dung and then started to sharpen his Green River knife. Satisfied with its edge, he fixed a piece of tin mirror in the loose bark of a tree.

At last Higgins asked, "What in hell you aimin' to do?"

"Mow the crop down."

"Shave? Jesus Christ! With that toad-stabber?"

"Done it many's the time."

"Why?"

"Don't like to be called dog face. That's Indian for whiskers."

"You wasn't always so tidy."

"Them west-coast Indians don't count."

"They was mostly pretty smooth-faced, though."

"Yup. Indian face skin can't grow much of a crop. If a hair happens to come through, the Indians pluck it out."

"Goin' to braid your hair, too?"

"Maybe. When it gets long enough."

"Well, let me borrow some of that hot water and soap. I got my own razor."

That night they let the campfire burn out, the air being soft with a touch of breeze in it. The horses grazed close, Feather's bell sounding clear to his step. Summers got the jug out and passed it, and they drank while butted on the ground by the dead fire.

Higgins looked up at the sky, at what he told himself was a glory of stars. "You ever see so many stars, Dick?"

"Wait till we get out on the plains."

"You ever tried to count 'em?"

"Sure did. But when I got to a million, I kind of dozed off. Take another swaller and pass the jug."

The liquor eased the ache in the bones and brought the mind to a sort of lazy life.

"What men may be doin' seems no account here," Higgins said. "Don't amount to a damn. But back in Missouri they was talkin' hot about war with Mexico so's to get Texas. What we want with Texas, Dick?"

"I never been there. Down south to Taos and around, but Texas wasn't for trappers. Put it the other way round. What does Texas want with us for a fact? Either way don't make sense, I'm thinkin'. We take it, and what do we get? More people, and we got a God's plenty of people. That's what spoils a country."

"All of us guilty, I reckon. I humped a little slave gal for a while. She was young, no older'n a yearling by animal count, but I never hung around to see what come of it. When it come to couplin', I can tell you, she was plumb human. That's what gets me about slavery. Countin' niggers no good except for work, then havin' a high old time with their heifers. You ever owned a slave, Dick?"

"Never wanted to."

"Me, neither. But if it ever got down to war, what would you do?"

"Cuss both sides probably. I don't know."

Summers fell silent. When at last he spoke, his voice sounded sad. "I seen this country in its prime, Hig. Beaver in every stream. We found passes, we did, and followed trails only game knew. But, hell, I jabbered about all this before."

"Not so plain as now. Go on."

"Where we set foot we might have been the first man there, and we breathed new air into our lungs, and all the time felt glad and free inside and never gave a thought about what was to come. About farmers and plows and hide-hunters and all that. We figured our life was forever. We screwed ourselves, me included, finding trails and passes and kind of gentling the country. It makes a man cuss himself."

"And that's why we're goin' where we're goin'?"

"One reason. To see what's left. To pleasure ourselves while we can."

A star fell down the sky, and the breeze stirred the ash of the fire, and Summers said for good-night while he looked up, "More damn people than all the stars."

They corked the jug and went to their beds. A bird, a jay maybe, squawked from the dark trees. Higgins lay on his back and let the stars and the night take him.

8

THAT HALF-BREED at the Dalles — yeah, Antoine was his name — knew what he was doing when he traced the way to the Bitter Root. Yet Summers figured he could have found it himself. A mountain man learned by the stream flow, by the game trails, by the lay of the land, by the hunch in his bones, how to get where he wanted to be.

Where he wanted to be was close to the mountains but out on the plains, where a man could look west and see the jagged wall that separated the worlds and east where distance ran beyond the reach of his eyes. He asked himself what he would do when he got there. Enjoy himself while the strength of his young time fluttered his bones. Enjoy himself. Sure. Chase down memories. It was as good a life as any he knew and better than most. Git along, hoss.

They were on a high tableland where trees were few and the wind could tear at them from any direction. A tumbleweed tore loose from its hold on earth and went rolling away. He had sand, the scourings of wind, in his teeth, in his ears and his clothes. The horses walked with their heads down, their manes and tails whipping. The torn air had the beginning bite of winter in it.

They had made good time, Summers thought while his horse shied at a tumbleweed that blew past his nose. They had tackled the trail early and late and kept going through all the days. They should be over the mountains and out on the plains before heavy snow fell, though no man could tell the way of the weather.

The trail led downhill and away, and from behind him Higgins shouted against the wind, "Holy Christ, what a slope!" There, down from them, was the Snake and its feeder, the Clearwater. Hard by was a shack and a horse corral. Both seemed deserted. Here, down in the hole, the air turned warmer. They held up, looking.

"If there was someone to home," Higgins said, his eyes on the shack, "we might pay a visit. Might hear some news."

"News don't matter to us, Hig. It's just talk where talk means nothin', just air passin' by."

"Might be more."

"Only if it's news of a war party, Injuns on the peck, and that ain't likely now, I'm thinkin'."

Higgins was a good man. He worked fine in harness. He did his full share of work. He didn't complain. And it was natural to him that he hankered to talk to somebody else. It was natural he asked questions there was no answer to. They didn't matter. They helped pass the time in camp.

At the bank of the Snake Summers held up again. "Looks like we could ford most anywhere. Some swimmin' water, but this ain't the Snake we knew before. It's calmed down a right smart. Let's move a piece, so's to land on the right bank of the Clearwater. That's where the trail is."

"Water's deeper there on account of the Clearwater comin' in."

"But not too bad, I bet you."

They dismounted a few yards downstream and loosened the cinches so the horses could draw in plenty of air and float lighter. Before they tried the crossing Summers asked, "How's your horses at swimmin'?"

"You seen them before. Like fish." Higgins gave his toothless grin. "You know. Under water."

A man couldn't call the ford bad. A place or two the horses had to swim, and the current carried them downstream a piece, but they climbed up on shore all right, and the packs hadn't suffered.

They waited for the horses to get their wind back. "Trail's over there, I figure," Summers said, "and we got a good part of the day left. What say we charge ahead if you're up to it?"

"Up to it, hell! Just keep out of my way."

The trail led into forests, into dense, tall stands of evergreens, some of which grew straight as a plumb line. Not all of the trees were the trees of Oregon. Some of them had different bark and different shape. The sun was lost here, crowded out, only a rare shaft slanting through the overhead growth. It wasn't land to a man's liking, not to his anyway, though there was no wet in the air and no salt. The wind had let up.

They found a small clearing and made camp just as dusk was closing in. They heated water and washed and shook the sand out of their clothes and put them back on again, for the night had turned chill. They ate deer meat that was going sour.

They lighted pipes afterward and sat and let the earth draw out their fag while they fed small bites to the fire.

"Reckon we're halfway to yonder?" Higgins asked.

"Couple of days, thereabouts, we ought to move down to the Bitter Root. Meantime we have to kill meat for the pot."

"Grouse likely. This ain't huntin' country. Too damn much growth. I can't hardly keep you in sight after you make a turn."

"Don't worry your head. We made out so far."

"That deer meat had a taint to it that don't rest easy in my belly."

"I'll find us an elk, I'm thinkin'. This is their kind of country."

"If you can see to aim."

In bed Summers heard the hoarse howls of wolves and the quavering cries of coyotes. He had to put his mind to it to hear them. They let loose every night and again just before sunup, and a man took them as natural as the sound of wind in the trees or of running water and didn't pay any heed, not unless he listened particular.

He wondered why they gave voice. Take a dog, now, and you could find reasons, like the barks were warnings or dares or came out of fear. But wolves? Coyotes? Did they cry out from hunger? From what was bred in them? For no reason that a man could put a name to? One thing for sure. They sounded lonely, like as if on lost trails.

He fell asleep to their howls and quavers.

The horses neighed shrilly. Hooves sounded and the breaking of brush. Feather's bell rang out wild.

Summers rolled from bed and grabbed his Hawken. As he moved out he felt rather than saw Higgins behind him. He moved by starshine. He squinted against the dark curtain of trees. There was a flowing movement like water in shadow, black sliding through black, and he fired, and a high scream chased the crack of the shot, chased other sounds into silence. He went on.

There, dying, lay a panther, shot through the chest. A star caught a golden gleam from the fur. The panther managed a snarl before its head fell.

"Cat country," Summers said as Higgins moved to his side. "Likely clawed one of the horses. Got to see."

They found Feather after a hunt. The other horses were close by. Feather's hams had deep slashes in them.

"Damn hobbles," Summers said. "They slowed him down. They was to blame."

"Not to mention the cat," Higgins said.

"Anyhow, the horses are glad for our company. No more hob-bles. After this they won't range far."

"Meantime, what do we put on them gashes?"

"Grease. Meat grease. Got any?"

"We ain't scoured the kettle yet."

"That'll do. Keep off the flies, come a warm spell. I don't look for poison to set in, not here in the mountains."

They doctored Feather as well as they could in the dark. One thing for sure, he had learned not to stray far from camp.

"Tomorrow," Summers told Higgins, "we'll have a go at painter meat."

"I hope God and my maw don't look on."

They went back to their bedrolls. Half-drowsing, Summers heard Higgins say, "And I thought I could shoot!"

9

THEY WERE NEARING the crest, so Summers told Higgins. "Another day or so," he had said, "and we ought to be hoofin' it down to the Bitter Root valley."

Higgins hoped so. He was tired of forests, tired of the trees that closed them in and even tireder of mountains. As they plodded along, his mind went to tracing the country they had come through. There was Oregon and the high trees and rain and moss and ferns and fronds where a horse went fetlock deep in the mold. There was the long plateau yon side of the Snake and wind that choked a man's breath in his lungs. And there was this long climb up the Clearwater and the damn forests again and a trail that turned tricky. How long had they been traveling? How far had they come? He asked Summers, and Summers answered, "Sleeps or miles?"

"I can figure the sleeps out for myself. Make it miles."

"I dunno. Three hundred plus, maybe. Maybe more. I ain't so much on miles. I go by country and seasons. Anyhow, we been makin' good time."

More than three hundred miles, and now it began to snow. There was wind with it, and the cold numbed fingers and feet, no matter the covering, and then it struck at the bones.

The snow whirled and played with the trail, more often hiding it than letting it show, and Summers pulled up his horse and shouted back, "Time to hole up, I'm thinkin'."

The wind swept the words away, swept them along with the snow into the moving trees, to the mountains and to hell and gone where.

Summers tried to look the country over. There was snow on his eyelashes, and he brushed it away. The horses stood hunched and sad. Summers set the string in motion again and led around to a small open space just beyond a stand of trees where the wind wouldn't hit them so hard.

They dismounted and set to work, Higgins helping to string a rope, tree to tree, and throwing the square of canvas over it. They tied and pegged the canvas and partly closed one open end with brush. There was wood to gather and a fire to be built. Summers got the fire going while Higgins brought in the wood.

Just seeing the fire was some comfort, Higgins thought. He brushed snow aside and spread a horse blanket to sit on. Who cared if the blanket stunk? He sat down, arms and legs outstretched toward the blaze. He could hear the horses pawing for grass and Feather's bell sounding.

They had brought a joint of meat in with them. To fingers still numb it felt frozen. The fire began to warm the makeshift tent.

Without speaking Summers went out and came in with the jug. "Whoever invented whiskey was thinkin' of times like these," he said.

"Want to send up a prayer for him?"

"I figure his sins is forgiven."

Summers passed the jug to Higgins, who drank and passed it back. "I'm hopin' there's no bottom to it."

"It's still better'n half full."

They roasted the meat over the fire after sampling the whiskey again.

Afterward Higgins said, "There's not enough wood to last the night out." He took the ax and started into the night.

"Watch out you don't get lost," Summers told him.

The cold took hold once he was outside. The wind walloped him, let up and walloped again, driving snow into his face. A man couldn't carry enough clothes to keep warm. He'd just give in like an overloaded pack horse. He bent his head and moved on, his feet sinking into a drift. Looking back, he could just see the tent, see it as a dim glow from the fire inside. He made two trips with wood and, shaking, sat down again by the fire.

He slept cold that night, even with most of his clothes on and the stinking horse blanket spread over his covers. He kept getting up to feed the fire. The cold didn't seem to bother Summers that much. Likely he was made of tougher stuff.

They got up at the edge of dawn. The wind had ceased but not the chill. Higgins hit at the tent where the snow had bellied it in. The snow slid off, being small-grained, each grain frozen.

Summers was putting on the capote that he had used over his bed. For all that he wore buckskins mostly, he put on boots, not moccasins. He yanked the coonskin cap down on his head. They had come to wearing the things in cold weather, Higgins having dug them out of a pack while saying, "My old man said, keep your head warm and your other parts will take care of themselves. He was half-right sometimes."

Summers said, "I'll see to the horses."

"Christ, Dick, we'll never find the trail in this snow."

"You think I'm a plumb fool?"

"I ain't never sure about you."

If they weren't sure-enough friends, Higgins thought, talk like that would sound sore. Higgins answered to Summers' grin.

"Loan me your scattergun, will you?" Summers asked. "Might see a chipmunk or something to shoot."

"If you don't, it's empty bellies today."

Summers went out. The horses couldn't be far away, not from the sound of the bell.

There was more wood to bring in, and another little item to attend to, like squatting in the snow. Higgins put on his capote and cap. His boots were stiff, of a mind, the damn things, to freeze his feet. He poked his hands into heavy gloves, grabbed a rag and went out.

Once away from the tent he put the gloves in his pocket and lowered his pants. God wouldn't ask a man to bare his ass as he had to. It was the devil at work. Finished he wiped himself with the rag and adjusted his clothes. He washed his hands and face in the snow and used the capote for a towel. The pile he had laid steamed behind him.

Like a fool, he had forgotten the ax. He went back and got it and set to work. While he was working, he heard one shot. One was all Summers ever needed. He was bringing in the last load just as Summers showed up.

"Horses all sassy," Summers said. He swung out a hand that held a rabbit. "One lousy snowshoe."

The sun was up now. It had no heat in it, only light, and a man could go blind from the glare on the snow.

Summers skinned and cleaned the rabbit and tossed it in a pot, ready for boiling. The tent had become fairly warm, warm close to the fire but chilly at the edges, so that a body felt half hot and half cold and kept squirming to thaw out the chilled parts.

"That sun might take on some meanin' later," Summers said, "but what we need now is more air."

Higgins took a deep breath and blew it out in a white plume. "I was just hopin' you could rustle up some."

"Air in the shape of more wind."

"Sure. I miss it."

"To scour out the trail. To lift up the snow. Sure, it will leave some drifts, but we can bull through."

"I'd as lief stay safe for a while as risk my neck."

"Risk is the name of it all, Hig. You can break a leg any time, get kicked by a horse, fall off'n a cliff, get lost and give up. But how'd you like to live without it, like a milk cow, say, or a prize stud horse? You want pamperin'?"

"Yeah. Like a woman to take the fret out."

"It's weather and chances we're talkin' about. The first snow goes away fast. You can bet on that."

Higgins put a stick on the fire. He looked through the open end of the canvas. "It's not meltin' now by a long shot."

"It's goin' away. Shrunk already by two inches or I'm a nigger."

"It's just settled, is all."

"That's not the half of it. This high up the air's pretty dry, and it sucks up the snow."

"I don't see any goin' back up."

"It evaporates. That's what it does. Goes up in a mist you can't see."

"Like the soul, huh?"

It was good to hear Summers laugh. Through the laugh he said, "Quit play-actin' the muttonhead."

With nothing else to do, they sat by the fire, lay down and snoozed, fed the fire and snoozed some more.

Half-drowsing, Higgins heard the wind again. The soul that went up in it would get one hell of a ride.

◥ ◥ ◥

Empty-bellied, they set out in the gray of morning. Summers had been right. The snow had shrunk, been blown away or gone up in mist. Or some of it had. Where it hadn't, the horses shuffled through, knee-deep in places. The wind had turned into a cold breeze. The red ball of the sun came up, cold-firing the snow. Higgins squinted and moved his cold butt in the saddle.

His life hadn't been worth a damn, he knew and didn't care. A man took things as they came and, if he had gumption, went out to meet what was coming. So he had thrown in with Summers and wasn't sorry. He wondered about the sadness he saw sometimes in Summers' face, a sadness that never poked through to sour his manner. He wondered if, like Summers, he had distance in his eyes, of long trails traveled and others that lay ahead. Summers had said risk was the all of it, but in his face, off-guard, was the look of search, of long wanting.

Anyhow, it was plod, plod, on and on, while the cold tried for a man's vitals and the breath of his horse came out frost. Times like these, it seemed a long way to yonder, but who wanted it underfoot?

Ahead of him Summers dismounted, his rifle in one hand. It was always with him, like a part of himself. He let the reins drop and went ahead, tramping a trail in a drift. Now Higgins saw why. The drifted snow slanted down to a drop-off, a cliff face with a base a hundred, two hundred feet down. A misstep or slip would shoot a man over the edge.

Higgins forgot he was cold. He raised his eyes from the drop. He tried to shut it out of his mind. Let him fall, he thought, looking up, and the mountains, dressed in starched white, would be his uncaring tombstones.

Returning, Summers said, "Better get off and lead your horse, Hig. Stay on the upside. It ain't so far."

Summers took Feather's reins and led away, walking careful. There was nothing for it but to follow his tracks. He kept his eyes on them. He hoped his horses were sure-footed. They ought to be, having four feet, if that didn't double the trouble. The horses followed readily enough, the dumb brutes.

Once past the drift, Summers held up and waited, his face smiling. "I was a mite scared we would roll the string," he said.

"I was scared we would roll me."

"You were, huh?"

"You ought to see what I got in my pants."

"I figure it's downhill and easier goin', here on out. Sun's warmin' up some, to boot."

"I hadn't took notice till now."

They pushed on, by and by leaving most of the snow. Summers' head was alert. He would be looking for meat. High time, too, Higgins' guts told him. But there wasn't any game, not even a track. And there weren't any birds in the trees.

Of a sudden Summers checked his horse and shot. He dismounted and walked off a piece and came back carrying some kind of animal.

"Bobcat," he said, "but it's meat. Don't usually see 'em in daylight."

He tied the cat to his saddle, mounted and rode on.

So it was on again the next morning with the pukey taste of cat meat in his mouth, and the sun turned kind and the snow went away and the breeze let up, and there was spring in the steps of the horses. Down, down, the trail turned, and now ahead lay a valley where the sun buttered the turned grass of meadow and slope. A river ran through it, fringed by cottonwoods and aspens and willows that hadn't yet lost their leaves.

"There's the Bitter Root," Summers said.

Higgins just looked, looked at the gentle valley and the leafed trees, feeling the sun as soft as a woman's touch. He called ahead, "And to think them people went clear to Oregon! Where's all the Indians?"

"Upstream by the mission, I reckon."

"Man, this is cozy. Just pitch a tent alongside the water and let time run by. It's a hellish temptation, Dick."

"Won't be that way for long. Someone will find it, and them that follers will ruin it. That's the way of things."

"The Flatheads haven't."

"Injuns don't. Got more sense."

"Right now, all I want is to go down to the river, get my tail out of the saddle and eat. I'm bound to say I ain't strong for what we been puttin' into our stummicks."

"Grouse tonight. Change of victuals. Let's get along."

Higgins brought in the grouse that afternoon, four of them, plump as fed chickens. Summers had unpacked the horses and now sat by the makings of a fire. He said, "Look off to your left, Hig."

A black bear stood there, its nose working. There was rust on its muzzle and paws.

"No harm in it," Summers said.

"Be a shame to shoot. Everythin's so tame, like friends. The grouse was more like tame hens. Tame fish in the river, too, I bet."

"Catch us a mess, then. I'll ready the grouse."

There was no trick to catching these fish. A man didn't even need bait. Just tie a bit of grouse feather to a hook and start casting.

Higgins gutted his catch and brought it in. Summers had a couple of grouse spitted over the fire.

"Fish, too?" Higgins asked.

"Sure thing."

"We got no grease for fryin'."

"Put water in the skillet, not too much. Poach 'em."

"If you ain't one smart son of a bitch!"

They followed the river down the next day and the next. It joined what Summers said had to be Clark's Fork of the Columbia. There Summers turned the string upstream. By and by they came to a great hole in the mountains, a giant deep saucer with peaks and high tumbles of hills for its rim. Mountains on all sides, some of them snow-capped, some of them thick with forest, but down here the weather was warm and the trees scattered more, and the river sang by, merry with its travels, and all a man wanted to do was to eat and sleep and let the sun shine on him. Someone would find this place, as Summers said, and others would be on his heels, but now this cupped world was all theirs, and the only tame sounds were the far-off barking of dogs in an Indian camp that Summers had sighted and sneaked them around, saying only, "I don't hanker for pipe-smoking and palaver, not now, though the Flatheads is peaceable."

Lying down in his bed that night, hearing the busy river, thinking of this valley in the high hills, Higgins told Summers, "Wake me up when the last trumpet toots."

10

THEY WERE OVER the Bitter Root, over Clark's Fork and well up the Big Blackfoot, the River of the Road to the Buffalo. Give them two more days, maybe three, Summers thought, and they'd spill out on the plains. Winter was holding off, and now he knew for a fact just where he was, though not once on the long trail from Oregon had he had to backtrack or correct course.

It was no more than the middle of the day, but Summers pulled up his horse and the string halted behind him. Here was a long, level open space, grassed, shrub-clumped and not thick with trees, and at its side flowed the Big Blackfoot, reduced now to stream size as the trail approached the divide.

"Hig," he said over his shoulder, "I'm thinkin' it would be smart to make camp and let the horses rest and fill up."

The horses were pretty gaunt, but, thanks to Higgins, there wasn't a sore foot in the bunch or a saddle sore. The claw marks on Feather's rump were healing up good.

"Suits me," Higgins said, "and will suit the nags even better, that's if they remember what full bellies feel like." His thin face screwed up as he studied the lay of the land. "We'll be needin' fodder our own selves."

"Name it. Deer. Elk. Maybe moose. I reckon you could catch us a mess of trout, if'n you feel like it."

Some aspen trees, still carrying a good half of their leaves, fingered down from a coulee, and they rode around them so as to have cover if the night wind blew. They unpacked and unsaddled the horses. The horses rolled, got up, sneezed and stepped off, feeding.

Higgins took a piece of rank meat from a pack and started cutting it in pieces for bait. His nose twitching, he said, "Fur as I know fish can't smell." Bait, fish line and hooks in his hand, he went on, "I'll cut me a pole down by the river."

Summers watched him as he made off. A man wouldn't think there was any strength in that long, scrawny body or any push. He wouldn't think so, and he'd be surprised. Like as not, Higgins would catch some fish. He usually did what he set out to do.

Summers gathered wood for the night fire and set rocks around so's to nest it. Then he sat down and allowed himself a pipe of tobacco, taking note to tell Higgins, for what they had they shared, much or little. They'd gone mighty easy on the whiskey, too, though they might drink some tonight.

He felt ease in him, the ease of almost arrival, and with it a sort of unease. Would the high plains be as remembered? Would buffalo graze there and antelope bucket away and halt, curious, and the sun shine long, morning and evening, and the buttes rise clear against the painted sky? And if they did, would it be as it was once? Too often, things weren't what they were cracked up to be. He let himself nap.

Higgins woke him up, Higgins coming into camp with a nice string of trout on a willow stick. "Nothin' to it," he said. "Gave up when my bait ran out. Ain't they pretty, though?"

Summers got to his feet. "They shine for a fact. My turn now. What'll it be?"

"Quail on toast, if it be so's to please you."

He didn't have to go far. With dusk closing in the deer were coming down to feed and water in this natural pasture. He lay behind a clump of brush and waited. A doe came first, her growing fawn behind her. They hadn't learned to be hunter-shy. They had only to watch for the big cats, wolves, and some-times a bear. Then came a plump doe — no fawn. She was a pretty thing, as delicate as, well as delicate as a she deer. She would be good to eat. He killed her with one shot from the Kentucky.

He went up to her, made his cuts and rolled out the guts, saving the liver. He was ready for Higgins when Higgins showed up with a pack horse.

That night they ate trout and deer liver, and Higgins said, cleaning up the last of it, "I swear it's better'n fat pork and mus-tard greens."

They scoured the pan, hung the carcass of the deer in a tree beyond the reach of bears and sat down by the fire.

Night had come on, clear and cold, and the stars glittered like mirrors touched by the sun. Coyotes and wolves were mak-ing their usual racket. Over a pipe Higgins said, "Nothin' like bein' footloose, pointed at nowhere in particular. Dick, was you always this way?"

"It's the way I'm aimin' to be, here on out."

Higgins took a pull on his pipe. It sucked in his lips where no teeth were. "Footloose and fancy-free, that's the sayin'. But I swear words is tricky things. What does it mean, fancy-free? Free of fancy? Free to hitch on to whatever one comes along? Free to follow what's already set in your mind?"

"I never gave it much thought." Summers drank from the jug

and passed it. He put a stick on the fire, thinking Higgins was talking just to be talking, talking because there was somebody to talk to, talking against the great loneliness that held and hurt a man.

"I don't know as it makes any difference," Higgins went on, wiping his mouth. "But a body likes to straighten things out in his mind. You wonder where the truth's at. Live and learn they say but don't say that all the while you're learnin' you're forgettin', too, until maybe at the last it's just a big forgettin'."

"Christ sake, swaller some more of that joy juice."

The fire glowed red, for now sending out heat enough. Overhead the cold stars danced as they had danced at Jackson's Hole, the Popo Agie and Horse Creek. That was a long time ago to a man but not to the stars. Their calendars were different. One star fell, making a quick streak in the sky, its seeing time ended.

"Quit beatin' your brain," Summers said. "Think on this. We been lucky. Lucky in the weather. Lucky in not bein' tormented and slowed up by Indians. Another time of year, and the Flatheads would be comin' or goin' on their hunts on the plains."

"It don't make much sense. They got all that pretty Bitter Root country to bang away in."

"But no buffalo."

"I know. You told me."

"A heap of fightin'. The Blackfeet didn't like that poachin' in the country they claimed."

"Still don't, I reckon."

"No, but smallpox took the starch out of them a few years back. Maybe half of them went under. I hear tell they're still mean but their pride's mostly gone."

Higgins fell silent, maybe still thinking about words and what they meant and all that. The whiskey wasn't doing what it should to him.

Summers sipped at the jug and went on. "I fell in with a party of Flatheads once, down there on the plains."

Higgins fed the fire.

"It was the spring hunt, and they brought with 'em some camas root. Man, what fodder!"

Higgins stirred himself enough to ask, "A treat, huh?"

"It tasted somethin' like a plum, but there they split up. It blowed you up fearful, more'n beans ever do, and when you broke wind the coyotes took off for fresh air. Magpies, comin' too close, fell dead out of the sky. The camp dogs puked, them as didn't give up the ghost."

Higgins was grinning.

"The Flatheads just laughed and kept fartin'."

"They just let 'er rip, huh?"

"Yup."

"Squaws, too?"

"These here was all men, but they wouldn't have paid no notice of squaws."

"Eatin' or whatever, they just let go. Right?"

"Yup."

"Feastin' and fartin'. They don't go together. It ain't nice. It's downright uncivilized."

"Natural, though." Summers took time to think out how to say what he wished to say next. "But what do you want, Hig, the fartin' few or the tight-assed many?"

Higgins jumped to his feet and saluted. "Yes, sir, general. I'm with you all the way, but I got to make bold to say we haven't the men or the arms to fight off what's comin'."

Summers had to laugh. "Sit down, soldier. We don't aim to fight them. The idee is just to go where they ain't."

"Just to get a taste of her, huh, before the flood laps her up?"

"Before she gets tamed."

"Suits me." Higgins sampled the whiskey and went silent again as if he had gone back to his earlier thoughts. A night bird called from the aspens behind them, and he asked, "What you reckon it is?"

"Just some little old bird, I reckon."

"Yeah, the bird in the bush, and that's another thing," Higgins continued as if talking to himself. "Take, now, a bird in the hand is worth two in the bush. That's true of the gut, but I got doubts for the spirit. The bird in the bush, it's always yonder and yonder. Right?"

"You frazzle things, Hig. Me, I'm goin' to bed."

Once in his bedroll Summers couldn't sleep. He heard coyotes and wolves, far off, and close at hand the voice of the night bird. The bird in the bush. Had he held it once, not knowing? Did it flutter there in his hand in those gone days, there along the upper Missouri, there in Jackson's Hole, there at rendezvous, where men drank and sang the old songs in young voices, and a squaw's eyes said yes, after a while? Where beaver swam in every stream, and a trapper knew his foot was first on the land and he walked with the gods of the world, knowing himself to be small and big and blessed and, ignorant, didn't give thanks, not full thanks, not until too late? Was the bird once in his hand, full-plumed, bright-colored, and had he let it slip from his grasp and fly on, calling him, its voice soft, its flame alive in the bushes, and when he went after it, it fluttered on, almost but not quite within reach?

That damn night bird called again. That damn Higgins was snoring.

❧ ❧ ❧

The frost lay silver on the grass when he woke up. It silvered the willows and the branches of the quaking asps. Low in the west a quarter moon was sinking. To the east the sky glowed red, showing the sun was on its way up. He rose and built a fire. It would be deer meat again, stabbed by sticks held over the coals.

Higgins lifted himself on an elbow and said, "Please to bring me coffee, black, and a platter of bacon and half a dozen fried eggs."

"No grits?"

"Goes without sayin'."

Higgins rolled out of bed and went to bring in the horses, his steps crunching the stiffened grass.

Packed up and mounted they followed the trail until the last of the Big Blackfoot seeped out in a swamp. There was no need to tell Higgins they were close to the big divide. Soon the going would be mostly downhill. Soon they would come to water flowing east. He whoaed up for a moment, long enough for Higgins to say, "You'd play hell gettin' a wagon over this pass."

Summers nodded and spoke to his horse.

Half a mile further on, where the trail bent around a rock ledge, Feather snorted and reared and wouldn't go on. Behind him the string started acting up. Summers slid off, reins in one hand, rifle in the other. He turned back, gave the reins to Higgins, shaking his head for quiet, and turned again, walking soft, the Hawken ready.

At first it was just a piece of fur, whitened at the tips. A step further and it became the biggest bear he had ever seen. It lay spraddled and quiet on the trail, dead maybe. Then he saw the great body rise and fall to its breathing. He skirted around it, ready to shoot. He hit it with a small rock. The bear didn't move. Then he saw that it lacked most of a foreleg. The stump oozed slow blood.

He walked back to Higgins and said, "Come on. Back a piece and tie up. Then follow along."

A little way off was a tree, and they wrapped reins around a couple of branches. "Need my gun?" Higgins asked.

Summers patted the stock of the Hawken and led off.

Higgins sucked in his breath as they rounded the turn. He wheezed out, "God! Good God!"

"Lost a foreleg above the second joint."

"Bled to death?"

"Still breathing."

"You goin' to put him out of his misery?"

Summers got down on one knee, resting his Hawken on the other. "Ephraim. Old Ephraim," he said.

"How's that?"

"I call to mind —" He didn't go on. He called to mind old days with the beaver traps, and young men, the traps lifted, sitting around campfires, and they would speak of Old Ephraim, the great white bear, and their tones held respect and awe and a sort of love, as if Ephraim somehow was a part of them, a living marker of the wild life they lived. Old Ephraim.

"He don't belong here," he said. "He belongs out on the plains. Drove here, that's what."

"But here he is. So what?"

Summers went on, "That Lewis and Clark party, now, they kilt ten of them by the great falls of the Missouri. Why? Why in hell?"

"You goin' to pray over him, Dick, or get it over with?"

"It ain't right. Why don't they leave him alone?"

"I never heard you take on over a critter, and him nigh onto dead."

"It's not just the one I'm thinkin' on. It's the whole breed, the whole goddamn family. What can you say later on? 'Yep, there was grizzlies in them days? There was Ephraim. You should have seen him.'"

"That ain't helpin' this bear."

Summers rose and handed his rifle to Higgins. "Keep a bead on him. You never can tell."

He walked back to the horses and took an old bucket from a pack. At a seep of water he made a hole with the bucket and filled it.

"Be damn ready to fire," he told Higgins on his return. "This here's a mite chancy."

He walked soft to the head of the bear and splashed it with water. No action. He began to pour slowly. At last a tongue came out and licked and licked again.

He walked back to the hole he had dug and refilled the bucket. He stopped by the horses and took a haunch of the deer he had shot the night before.

Higgins stood silent, the rifle steady.

Summers put the full bucket down and with it the haunch of deer. To Higgins he said, "We'll go back to where we was. Good day to do up the washin'."

He felt Higgins' eyes on him as they returned to the horses. He heard Higgins say as if to himself, "This here is crazy. A rare sparrow, that's you, Dick Summers."

Yeah. Hig might be right.

11

SUMMERS kept his horse to a fast walk, feeling clean for once and freshened by cleanliness. They had washed out some clothes and greasy rags the afternoon before, flopping the things in the river current and slapping them on rocks. At least the smell went out of them.

Afterward they had bathed, in water cold enough to curl a man's hair, not to mention other parts, and stood on the bank, shivering, and let the weather dry them.

Higgins had asked, "How in hell did the mountain men keep clean?"

"Mostly, they wasn't too tidy. From fall freeze to spring thaw they molded in their clothes, unless the weather was good enough to set traps. Then they got wet leastwise."

"I bet they stunk."

"They had all outdoors to stink in."

Now they were nearing the spot where they'd seen the big bear. "Watch sharp," Summers said. "I ain't lookin' for a charge, but you never can tell."

"I'm bettin' he's dead."

At the turn in the trail the horses began acting up, though not so much as before. Summers spoke to Feather and kicked him on. The bear was gone and so was the meat they had left. The bucket lay in a bush.

"You lose your bet," Summers said. "He drank and et and got up, and like as not is layin' somewhere close. Keep your eye peeled." He slid from his horse, handed the reins to Higgins, took a forequarter of the doe he had shot and laid it in the trail. Then he picked up the bucket and tied it on.

"You takin' on another mouth to feed?" Higgins asked. His face was squinched up, in disagreement or thought.

"It won't hurt, for the time bein'."

They rode on and came, at about the middle of the day, to a tiny stream where they let the horses drink.

"Notice anything?" Summers asked.

"Not what I ain't seen before."

"The water's flowin' east. We're over the hump, hoss."

"What I taken notice of," Higgins told him, "was them choke-cherries. Leaves mostly dead, but there's them berries, black, ripe and ready. What say we tie up and try a few? Been a long time between fruits."

They filled their mouths, blowing out the seeds through the tunnels they made with their tongues. After he had satisfied himself, Summers took out his knife and cut a bundle of loaded branches. He laid them on the trail, knowing that Higgins was shaking his head.

"I figure," he said, coming back, "that Old Ephraim would have a hard time, strippin' branches with only one paw."

"That damn bear ha'nts you."

Perhaps it did, Summers thought. Perhaps he was playing the

fool. But there was that other time, there were those other times, those other Ephraims, those other nights under the moon, and a man, looking sharp, might see the bear standing at the far edge of light, a curious onlooker at the doings of men.

"I want he should build up his strength," he told Higgins. "He's bound to follow the grub trail, and I don't like the idee, him on my ass forever."

"Now, not forever, Hig. Pret' soon, he'll hole up for the winter, and he needs meat on his bones and food in his belly for the long sleep. And he ain't goin' to hurt you nor me. I'm thinkin' he knows his friends, that I am."

Higgins grunted but managed a smile before he mounted his horse. "You're a damn notionable man. Some would say soft."

"Some have."

"And learned better?"

"Maybe a few."

Before too long, Summers thought, they would ride out of the mountains, and the eye would ramble while the west wind blew soft, and the lungs would fill with air that was better than liquor in the belly. Yet he felt a little like holding back, like waiting, like wanting certainty.

He straightened in the saddle, knowing that muzzling over what might be had dulled his senses. Approaching them, a rifle in his hand, was a man on horseback.

The man rode slow, squinting for better sight, one hand fast on the rifle. At last he raised a hand and called out, "How-de-do there, gents."

Summers lifted an arm and said, "How."

"I couldn't tell was you Injuns or not," the man told them as he approached. "It's them ring-tailed caps. Look like braids."

Summers sat silent. So did Higgins behind him.

The man had a red face and a belly that hated a belt. He had gear on his saddle — a bedroll tied behind the cantle and stuff in the saddle pockets.

"My name's Brewer. People call me Hank," the man went on.

"I'm tryin' to search out the biggest goddamn bear a man ever see. You spot any blood on the trail?"

"Blood?" Summers said, turning toward Higgins. "I don't recollect any blood. How about you?"

"Nary a drop."

"It was like this," Brewer said. "I was huntin' buffalo, two or three days down the line, and I seen this here monster and fired. Hit him, too. He made off into the bushes with a foreleg floppin'."

Summers asked, "When?"

"Four, five days ago. I figured it best to let him stiffen up or bleed himself weak and not tackle him fresh-wounded. But I had a time, then, findin' enough buffalo to keep my skinners busy. That's what held me up. Mainly, that is." The man's smile had a hungry and remembering look. "I wasted time yesterday tryin' to make up to a squaw. Damndest thing. There she was, alone except for a young'n, camped in a coulee and kind of hidden away. You know how a man gets away from women. Hard up, that's what I was. So I begged like and, bein' a fair man, offered a blanket and even some money, and all the time she held an old musket pointed straight at my gut. Crazy, I call it."

Brewer looked at Summers for approval. "But that ain't here or there. It's the bear I'm after."

"Judgin' by the bore of that rifle, you could shoot a horse turd through it and not grease the barrel," Summers said.

Brewer patted the rifle's stock. "I had it made to order, my order, and, by God, you shoot a critter with it any old place and down it goes."

"Too bad it don't shoot straight."

"Now how come you say that?"

"It was a big target, that bear, sayin' he was as big as you make out, but the shot got him just in the leg."

"The bear was movin', and the size of him gave me the fidgets. Not the fault of the rifle."

"So you aim to finish him off?"

"Course."

"Why?"

"So I can say I kilt him, the biggest grizzly any man ever seen."

"You could say that regardless, I'm thinkin'."

"Sure, but no proof."

"You'll need another horse to carry the hide."

The man looked into the distance, then back at Summers. "I hadn't give thought to that," he said. "But likely I could butcher his head off or hack out some teeth to back me up."

After a silence Higgins joined the talk. "You say huntin's poor, buffalo huntin'?"

"Puny. Buffaloes mostly has drifted south with the season. No big herds. With a big bunch a man can shoot ten or maybe forty from one stand."

Summers said, "That's mighty interestin'. I never heerd the like of it." He made his tone mild against the dislike that was in him.

"It takes a good eye, but about that bear. I found blood on the trail yesterday and maybe a spot or two today."

"If it was him for a fact," Summers said, keeping his voice soft, "I figure he circled around you and went on out, likely makin' for a swamp. You take a grizzly and wound him, and if he don't charge he'll make for a swamp every time. He can cool his hurt there and feed on cattails and such. There's cool and cure in swamp water."

Brewer straightened in his saddle. "Maybe so, but I figure I'll go on a piece anyhow."

Summers shook his head. "It's up to you. What say, Hig?"

"Every man's got his rights, right or wrong."

"What are you sayin'?"

"Don't mind us, mister."

"What in hell is it?"

"Injuns." Summers spoke to Higgins. "How many was there, hoss?"

Higgins was quick to catch on. "Ten by my count. Young bucks."

"Damn Blackfeet."

"Oh, now, Dick," Higgins put in. "They wasn't too bad. They let us through, didn't they?"

"On account of I know some Blackfoot talk. On account of the tobacco they took off'n us."

"And the jug. I was forgettin' the jug."

"That firewater will set 'em off."

"Maybe not. What you tryin' to do? Just faze the man?"

The man, Summers could see, looked fazed. "Me, I wouldn't keer to meet 'em again."

"If they're there," Brewer said, saving his pride, "the bear won't be nowhere near. Where were they bound?"

"This way when they finish the jug."

"I ain't a coward, but no man alone wants to meet up with a war party. Right?"

"Right."

"How about just trailin' along with you?"

"Three of us might set 'em off," Summers said. "Best you go ahead. We'll laze along, kind of a rear guard. Worst comes to worst, we got another jug."

Brewer nodded, turned his horse around and kicked it to a brisk walk. Turning back for an instant, he called, "If you do any good with that squaw, hump her one for me."

When he was out of earshot, Summers told Higgins, "Our play-actin' sure shot him down." He grinned into Higgins' grinning face.

"Take a bow, man."

"Take one yourself."

"No fools, no fun. That's what I say."

"What I say is, let's find a nice place to camp."

12

SUMMERS was in no hurry. They had made it over the Bitter Roots and over the Rockies, and a day or two more would see them out on the plains. He stretched in his bed, hearing Higgins fussing around camp. It was good just to lie thinking, to hope to see the trapping grounds again and the clean streams that joined the Missouri, to see space without limit or people to claim it and dwarf it.

Like he told Hig, it wasn't that he disliked people. Taken singly or in limited bunches, they were all right. He wasn't by nature like some he could name, men who distrusted strangers and hated settlements, who shied away from all law, who took up with squaws and abused and deserted them and went on, ready with knife or gun at the hint of an insult. Yet he wondered.

No. He was on the wrong trail. It wasn't crowds so much that disturbed him. It was what crowds meant, what settlement meant.

For now he just rested, and a small fear was in him, the fear of what he might find. Things changed, himself included. Would the plains look as they once had? Seeing, would his chest swell again? Memories could play a man false. Could he see through the eyes that were young once?

Well, enjoy the now time. It wouldn't come again, though likely he would wish it to. Think of Higgins and his fiddle and the song he'd made up on the trail. He heard it again, heard the music of the fiddle and Higgins' clear voice, sometimes singing, sometimes just reciting to the bare touch of the strings. He had asked Higgins to run through it again, so's he'd remember. He heard it now, tone by tone, word by word, and saw Higgins, sawing and singing in the light of the campfire.

> I met up with the Bitter Root
> On a warm and sunny day.
> It met me with a friendly hand
> And said, "Please, stranger, stay."
>
> Oh, my wanderin' soul.
> Oh, my wanderin' soul.
> Why can't it settle down?
>
> Then came another pretty place.
> Clark's Fork it was by name.
> I said, "I'm pleased to meet you."
> It said, "To you the same."
>
> Oh, my wanderin' soul.
> Oh, my wanderin' soul.
> Why can't it settle down?
>
> My pardner says keep goin'
> Beyond the mountain range.
> "No tellin' what we'll find there,
> But it will be a change."

Oh, my wanderin' soul.
Oh, my wanderin' soul.
Why can't it settle down?

My pardner says, "Make tracks, hoss.
From country that's too mild.
It'll draw the white man sure, hoss.
He'll have it quick with child."

Oh, my wanderin' soul.
Oh, my wanderin' soul.
Why can't it settle down?

Now I'll tell you why and which,
And there we'll let it be.
I'm pardnered with a son of a bitch
Who has the itch,
The self-same itch as me.

◖ ◖ ◖

Summers laid another chunk of meat on the trail. There was
enough left for supper and breakfast. Next day he'd shoot more
for the pot. The way was mostly downhill now, falling away
through the mountains to open country. The sun was halfway
down from its high point when Higgins called ahead. "I got a
feelin' we're bein' follered. I got a hunch, Dick."

"Likely so," Summers answered, speaking what he thought
was maybe true.

"And here I am at the tail of the string. Bait, that's what I
am."

"Act pretty, then. Swell up. Ephraim don't go for stringy
meat."

"Good. He'll pass me up and go for you, you puss gut."

"Just send him on."

The trail fell away and climbed, and there, beyond the tum-
ble of foothills, soft in the sun, spread the plains. Summers
pulled up. It was a flung land, he thought, a land broadcast by
the first hand from the raw beginnings of earth. There were the

buttes, standing ragged in the light, and the levels that led to the end of the world. There was a stream with its border of growth, bound down to meet the big river. There against the far skyline were shapes that were buffalo. Here Boone Caudill had roamed.

A wind came up from behind him. It blew his hair before his eyes and went on to ruffle the yellowed grass.

He pushed the hair from his eyes and said, "Blackfoot country, Hig. Crow country south and east."

Hig answered, "Your country, Dick."

13

THEY MADE CAMP that night in the foothills by the side
of a creek that Summers felt sure was a fork of the Dearborn. It was strange country to him, strange in the sense
that he had never been right here before, but familiar because
it was of a piece with country he knew.

Lying awake, he saw Old Charlie again, tracing water
courses in the sand with a forefinger as they sat by the night
fire. "It was purty country, that Dearborn stretch was, purty as
this nigger ever saw, that's what it was, and beaver in every
bend of her, but here, along nigh to sundown, come the Blackfeet, a party of 'em, and this child come close to losin' his hair.
Would have wasn't it for a fast horse. Arrers singin' past me
like birds and one took me in the arm. We was just two, my
pardner and me, and we lit out, sayin' one day we'd traipse

back and git our traps, but we never did, that we didn't."

Old Charlie had been rubbed out by the Arapahoes a year later, and the traps would be long rusted now or lifted by other hands, and all that was left was the trapper's remembered words. Summers fell asleep hearing them.

They ate a late and scanty breakfast and rode on until Summers spotted three bighorn sheep on a ridge above them. He slipped from his horse. They were almost within rifle shot. He sneaked closer, stooping for cover, and got a bead on the smallest one and fired. The target made one jump and began rolling down the hill toward him. For an instant the others stood, startled, and then ran from sight.

When he got to the dead sheep, he found Higgins by his side. Together they dragged it to the trail, bled and gutted it.

"Wisht I had a hunter's eye like you, Dick," Higgins said. "Good eatin', huh?"

"Next to buffalo by my thinkin'."

They started skinning, Summers telling Higgins, "See the wool don't touch the meat. Makes it taste sheepy."

"So my grandmammy told me down on the farm."

While he used his knife, Higgins asked, "You aim to look in on that squaw we heard tell of?"

Summers shrugged. "You gettin' ideas?"

"Curious is all."

"There's two ways to figure her. Either the tribe kicked her out or she flew the coop."

"Why would they kick her out?"

Summers shrugged again. "Maybe she couldn't keep her skirt down. Indians are funny about that, some of them are. If the man of the lodge agrees to it, then his woman can lay with somebody else. If she sneaks off on her own and he finds out, then he bobs off the tip of her nose."

"What if she does it again?"

"I dunno. Maybe they turn her out on the prairie."

Summers began wrapping the sheep carcass in a piece of canvas. He went on, "Maybe she was just too ornery. Wouldn't work, hands or tail either, though that strikes me unlikely."

"Or maybe she just run off, things bein' not to her taste."

"I reckon."

They roped the canvased meat on a pack horse, leaving the entrails and head on the trail. Looking at them, Higgins said, "If that brute of a bear is on our tail, he'll have him a feast. Figure he is, Dick?"

"Was you sick and hurt, wouldn't you follow the grub line?"

Higgins looked again at what they were leaving. "Not to eat guts."

They went down to the creek to wash their hands. Feather had learned to stand when the reins were dropped.

As they mounted, Higgins said, "My mind keeps goin' to that squaw."

"She sees your pecker, she'll shoot it off."

"She'll have to shoot fine."

Well, Summers thought, kicking his horse, why not see her? They weren't pushing to get any place in particular. He doubted, though, that Higgins would get what he wanted, not from a squaw who had pointed a gun at a man who wanted the same thing.

The sun moved in a sky that might never have known a cloud. The aspens glowed yellow but were dropping their leaves. Here and there chokecherries hung fat and black. The cottonwoods rose higher, naked as skeletons now. Here and there a dwarf pine hung to its hold on soil and rock. Except for the sounds of their gear there was silence around them, not an animal cry or a wing flutter. Overhead, an eagle soared, voiceless.

Feather lifted his head, his nose quivering. Off to the right was the beginning of a gulch where aspens grew. Summers looked for smoke but saw none. Neither did his nose find it. But a horse knew what a man might not. Summers turned in his saddle. "Visitin' time a-comin'. Put on your good manners."

They forded the creek and pushed through the growth that grew along it, and there, half-hidden, rose a tepee, and, in front of it, a woman who ran and picked up a gun. Behind her a child sat on a piece of old robe.

Summers halted the string when he had ridden closer. He said, "How." The woman stood unmoving, both hands on the gun. Even at this distance he could see it was an old fusee, probably a Hudson's Bay musket. He couldn't guess at the age of the woman though she was probably pretty young. Even in her hide sack of a dress he could tell she hadn't grown fat and squatty, as squaws did often with age. Her eyes were big, not crowded by high cheekbones, and her face was thin, made that way by nature or hunger. And damned if the child behind her didn't have red hair.

Summers dismounted slowly, propped his Hawken against a bush, and made the sign for peace, holding both hands in front of his body, the back of his left hand turned down.

The woman stood and looked, unmoving.

He didn't know the sign for meat, if there was one, and instead went to a pack horse and took the wrapped-up sheep. As he did, Higgins said softly, "She's like to shoot you."

"Them old smooth bores ain't so scary."

He carried the meat toward her and unwrapped it and stood, then closed his hand and brought it in front of his body, his forefinger pointing up in the sign for "come."

She didn't come. She stayed where she was, looking at him puzzled and questioning, as if there were more to him if she could bring it to mind. Then she lowered the musket and said, "How."

Summers carried the meat to her, saying over his shoulder, "You mind unpackin' the horses, Hig, and takin' 'em to grass? No bell on Feather. Just hobbles. This is Blackfoot country."

She was Blackfoot herself, he felt sure. One thing, her moccasins didn't match. By the fire were a couple of knives and a kettle. Keeping the meat on the canvas, she carved off pieces, knowing how, and pitched them in the kettle. From a hide bucket she added water. The child behind her sniffed like an animal. He cocked an ear to listen. He might have been a fox. Summers saw then that he was blind.

"Know white man's talk?" Summers asked as she worked.

She studied what he had said, the knife uplifted, as if to find meaning in each word. Then with her free hand she brought her thumb against her forefinger until only a bit of it showed. That was the sign for "little."

In Blackfoot, he guessed, she asked what he knew of her tongue, and he answered as she had.

Higgins came from unpacking and loosing the horses. "Gettin' anywhere?"

"Gettin' to a meal."

"Her nose ain't been bobbed, anyhow. Jesus Christ, Dick, that young'n's blind."

"I took notice."

"How they make out, you reckon?"

"Not too fat, I'm thinkin'. Likely she sets snares for rabbits and maybe grouse. Close up, she could kill a critter with that old musket."

Summers started to make a fire, but the woman waved him away. All right. She was boss of her own household.

The child set up a thin wail like a bird peep in the great silence. She quieted him with a pat on the head and a sound in her throat. He couldn't have been more than three years old and maybe not that.

She had the fire going now. Young sheep didn't take long to cook.

Summers sat back on the ground and with a twig from the fire lighted his pipe. The real warmth of the day was over. Shadows of the mountains were growing over the camp. Pretty soon the coyotes would tune up. The woman took something from a small leather sack and added it to the stew.

They ate with knives and their fingers, spearing pieces of meat and letting them cool. When the piece was too big a mouthful, Summers used his knife to cut the bite off in front of his nose. He saw Higgins watching him.

On a scrubbed stone the woman cut small chunks and fed them to the child. Between bites the woman said, "Plenty good." It was the first English she had spoken.

After eating they washed their hands and mouths with water from the hide bucket. There was nothing to dry them on, nothing but the soft air and the breeze that had sprung up.

Higgins said, "Ain't she got horses? I didn't see any."

Catching her eye, Summers made the sign for horse and raised his eyebrows. She held up two fingers.

"Yep," Summers said to Higgins. "Two. They're hid away somewhere."

Night came on, and Summers rolled out his bed, not close to the tepee. Higgins did the same.

There was wind in the mountains, wind in the high tree tops, but here they lay snug, hearing the long voice of it. Sure enough, the coyotes started their hill-to-hill chorus, wind song and coyote song and silence hanging over them both. And who was this squaw, camping alone with her child? How come and why? It wasn't her looks that had set her apart from her tribe. That was for sure. Had she fled from it for reasons unknown? Would she go back? Would they, he and Higgins, stay around for a while? There were questions and questions and no answers that came to mind.

Higgins said, "You reckon, Dick? You reckon now that we've got acquainted?"

"This nigger wouldn't try it. Just go to sleep."

He drowsed off seeing the woman, seeing her slim and big-eyed, her look puzzled, and seeing the blind child, too, the red-headed child. Some white man had got to her all right. The hoarse howls of wolves joined with the cries of coyotes.

Higgins woke him up, Higgins breathing loud and shuffling again into his bed. As if to himself Higgins said, "I be good goddamned!"

"Told you so."

"I wasn't forcin' myself on her, Dick. You know I wouldn't. I just stood by the tepee flap and made what I thought was coaxin' sounds, and the flap flew open, and there was the damn musket pointed at my belly button and her holdin' it. So I made tracks."

"I reckon you're wilted down."

"Shrunk to nothin'."

"So forget it and go back to sleep."

Summers chuckled to himself. For no reason at all he felt pleased.

14

SUMMERS was ready with two pack horses when the slow sun came up. They had eaten at first light, and the woman had cleaned up afterward and had turned to scraping the sheep hide while the child sat sampling whatever smells the breeze brought. Now there was nothing for him to do but take off.

Higgins stepped to his side. "Any orders for me, general?"

Higgins was a knowing man. He understood without being told that Summers wanted to be alone for a while. Still, it seemed kind of unfair.

"You could go down along the creek, I'm thinkin', and shoot some ducks. Ought to be some teal and mallard in the potholes. Bring back plenty meat, me."

"You ain't talkin' to an Injun now."

Summers smiled at him. "I aim to get us a buffalo. The woman will dry some of it and maybe make pemmican and have something to tide her over the winter." Summers mounted Feather and got the outfit moving.

The night had brought frost, but it was melting now, and, touched by the sun, the tops of the grasses trembled with light. Tiny pieces of mirrors, Summers thought, each flashing a message if a man could read it.

He rode down a long hill and up and down another, and the plains spread before him, sharp in the sun, and a butte rose and another, and a small bunch of antelope, taking silly fright, bucketed a few yards and stopped, their rumps showing white. Once antelopes were called goats, he remembered, which was a put-down on the breed. An antelope was pretty fair eating, what there was of it. He knew he could bring them within shooting distance. Just get away from the horses, lie down, hold the rifle up with a tatter of flag on it, and curiosity would do the rest.

He went on, letting the air and the sky and the earth sink into him. It was more than the lungs that this country filled. It was the eye and the spirit and the whole of the body from topknot on down. How many times had he just sat and looked? How many times, seeing, had he felt part and partner of what he saw? Never enough times. Each time was a new time, born fresh from the old, close kin to it, showing likeness, but still new.

He passed through a thin thicket. Off to his left was an old buffalo bull, its beard touching the ground. An old bull, standing alone, cast out from the herd, horned out by younger ones and left to remember the cows he had covered and wouldn't again. The bull raised its great head and stared at him, its eyes sullen and sad. Soon enough the wolves would disable it and, first thing, eat its balls off. Small loss, considering.

He raised a hand and said to the bull, "Too bad, old-timer." He led the string on. It wasn't the blue meat of an old bull that he wanted to bring back to camp.

Over a swell of land he saw what he wanted — a dozen or so buffalo in a hollow. They were the leavings of the great winter migration to the south, some of the few that voted to stick where they were. No bulls among them but one early-born calf, too young to show much of a hump. The bulls, along with the big herds, would come later and make thunder in the rutting season with their bawlings and pawings.

Summers tied Feather to a clump of brush, not trusting him to stand ground-tied here. He pushed ahead, stooping, then crawling, until he was within range. He didn't shoot yet. He just lay there. Once he had found sport in killing things. That was when the world was young. Now he shot for the pot, or was about to. But men still hunted for sport. Men hunted for money. To hell with both kinds! The one right a man had was killing for food.

A fly, on wing when it shouldn't be, touched his nose and buzzed on. A pattern of wild geese honked overhead. He listened to the lost, brave sound and his eye settled on a rattlesnake, soaking up the sun four or five jumps away. It was too dull to know it was there out of season. It just answered to warmth.

It was time to shoot, he knew. He had even picked out the target — a young, fat cow. He listened to the fading calls of the geese and watched the snake and lay still.

When the buffalo began to move off, he fired, and all the still day was shaken. The sound of the shot rolled through the hills and was thrown back by the mountains. The snake coiled and rattled.

The cow fell over. The others smelled the blood, not understanding, and stood dumbly about until Summers rose to his feet. Then they galloped away.

Summers recharged his rifle. That was the first rule of the country. Keep your gun loaded. Then he walked back and brought up the horses. He bled the cow. Skinning was a considerable job, best done, he thought, before he opened the carcass. He tied a rope to his saddle horn and used Feather to help pull off the hide. He cut through the belly tissue and raked out the entrails. With his knife and a small ax he quartered the meat, wrapped it, lashed it to the pack horses and started for camp.

It had taken longer than he expected. The sun had begun to slant from the west. A gust of wind came at him, blowing sand with it, and he had to wipe grit from his eyes. There now was the tepee and the woman at the fire, Higgins standing nearby, the child sitting. At the creek he washed his hands and forearms, using sand for soap.

At the camp the woman came up, expecting to unpack the horses. Summers gave her a look and said, "No." She went back to the fire.

Higgins stepped close to help. He said, working with a rope, "That squaw is as queer as fur on a snake. Won't let a man do nothin', not even rustle up firewood. Wants to do it all by her damn self. What's the reason for that, Dick?"

"Trainin'. Squaws for the camp work, men for the hunt."

"Nice, if you like slaves. I got the best of her, though. I shot ten ducks and picked and cleaned them myself, out of her sight. She looked at me like I had two heads, both empty, but she's cookin' the birds now."

They turned one pack horse loose and shooed it away.

It was then that Feather nickered. It was then that the child cried a thin cry.

Summers' eyes went from his work. Coming toward them, yon side of the fire, were four mounted Indians. He said, "Stay back, Hig. My move."

He stepped toward the Indians. The campfire was between them. The woman had turned her back to attend to the child. Summers slanted his rifle against a bush and made the peace sign. He said, "How."

They were young bucks, not feathered or painted, and Summers guessed they were out to steal horses, hoping maybe to spot a Crow camp. They jerked their horses to a stop and sat silent and unmoving. Summers said, "How," again.

A tatter-ass bunch, Summers thought, tatter-ass but danger-
ous. Their saddles were wooden, hacked from tree trunks and
cushioned by pieces of fur. Their bridles and bits were single-
rein braided hide. Bows and arrows hung from the saddles and
fastened to one was a heavy musket. It might be, it could be,
an old Harper's Ferry, brought west by the Iroquois or Dela-
wares that Hudson's Bay had employed.

Watching them, Summers almost wished that he had his rifle
in hand.

The lead man held a bow and arrow. He got off his horse and
put them aside. The buck behind him dismounted, too. The
others remained on their horses, probably told by word or sign
to do so.

The first man said, "How." The one behind him pushed forward. He was a muscled young buck with the show, Summers
thought, of the animal in him.

The second man looked around and saw the woman, her back
still turned. He strode forward and yanked her around and then
slapped her face hard, saying something that sounded like "No
Man Woman."

On their own Summers' legs moved. Of itself his arm swung.
His hand smacked against the Indian's cheek and knuckled it
on its return.

The Indian's face showed shock, then glowing anger. He ran
to grab for Summers' rifle. Higgins stepped from behind a pack
horse, the Kentucky steady in his hands. He said, "Hold it right
there."

The horses began rearing and plunging, their eyes white with
fright. Before the Indian could clutch Summers' rifle, his mouth
fell open.

It wasn't Higgins or the Kentucky that did it. It was Old
Ephraim, raising his great shape, standing as high as a mounted
rider. Summers swiveled. The other Indians had clapped their
hands over their mouths. The men on foot managed to catch
and mount their horses. The four of them galloped away, their
voices hoarse. Ephraim let himself down and went out of sight.

Summers dropped to the ground and laughed.

Higgins, stepping close, said, "Close shave, and you're gigglin'."

"Old Ephraim, he won the war."

"They scared mighty easy."

"Not to their way of thinkin'. He was medicine, bad medicine, our medicine, standin' there tall with only one paw on him. Jesus!"

Summers rose to his feet. The woman was at the fire again. Her face showed the mark of a hand. "Leave a front quarter on that pack horse, Hig," he said. "Ephraim has done sung enough for his supper."

He rode out in the direction from which the bear had come. He left the meat a quarter of a mile away from camp. He watched but didn't see Ephraim.

The night chill was coming on when he got back to camp. They ate duck and a chokecherry paste the woman had ground up.

The moon swelled on the eastern skyline, orange-red, ten times the size it would shrink to. Higgins, digesting his supper, had run out of words. It was just as well. Words clouded things, misting the moon, holding up the good feel of the breeze, mixing wrong with the cries of coyotes.

It came on to bedtime or nigh to it. The woman had gone to her tepee, taking the child with her. The boy could walk but didn't dare to without his mother's hand in his. His name, she had said, was Nocansee, which sounded Indian but wasn't when you spaced it out. Summers smoked and let time slide by.

When he looked at the tepee again, he saw the woman standing there, outlined, shining in the moonlight. Her gaze was on him. She made a bare movement with her head. So it had been before. So it had been with the Rees and Shoshones when he was young.

He rose and moved toward her, and the tepee flap closed slowly, and Higgins said, "Christ sake."

The child was asleep, and she was under a robe when he entered. Without words he took off his clothes. She turned down the robe for him.

His hand found her bare skin and moved over and down. She smelled a little of woodsmoke, as he must smell himself, but mostly she smelled of clean, willing woman.

Desire rose hard in him, desire that he had thought dying or dead and didn't care much if it was. Not now, though. Not now.

She was moist and in-taking, and he felt loved by her tissues, and at the last she had clutched him and squirmed under him so as to give him the best of the last.

He lay with her head on his arm and heard the cries of the geese and the songs of coyotes and the wash of wild waters, and he was on the keelboat *Mandan* again, back in time by fifteen years, and the Missouri ran under them, coming from the Blackfoot country to which they were bound. And on board was a little Indian girl, a doll child with big eyes, and she was the daughter of a Blackfoot chief, so it was said, whom the *patron* had found in St. Louis after she had been stolen away from her parents. He would take her, the *patron* would, back to her father and so make sure of friendly and profitable trade with the tribe. But the girl, that wisp of a girl, had slipped away just before they got there.

He hadn't thought of her in a long time. Fifteen years gone by and all the trails traveled since then, the good years, the empty years, the fun had and the miseries endured, and friends dead and friends made while time flowed uncaring.

Her name fluttered at the edges of his mind and then came in, and he knew it could not be. Over this great reach of country for two to come together like this! It was as unlikely as walking on water, as two needles coming point to point in a haystack. But maybe there was some direction, some guidance, some reason unknown to him. Maybe it was just chance, but one thing for sure: there was magic in the world.

He said softly, "Teal Eye."

She put a hand over his mouth. "Me know. Dick Summers."

Part Two

———————◆———————

15

HALF a man's life, Higgins figured, was spent on a horse. Well, not half, but enough that riding came as natural as walking and made no call on the lungs.

He kicked his horse gently and pulled at the rope that led to the two pack horses. The pack horses had slowed with age and were likely to stumble. That was one reason for his trip — to see about younger ones.

It was early spring. The wild geese had flown north, honking their way through the skies. Wherever water was, the ducks had paired off, the males bright in their courting clothes. No flowers yet, but the first shoots had poked through the warming soil. On the plains the blooms would grow low, knowing the wind. Only the armies of grass dared to stand very high.

He turned and looked back. There was the wooded valley of

the Teton River, their home for more than three seasons now. It was better country for game, for buffalo, than the upper Dearborn. Sure, they had made a few sashays out from it, but it still was home. Four Persons was the name of the place, so Teal Eye had said, because four Crows had been killed in the valley. He took a last look, seeing their tepees snug on the far bank of the stream. Against the skyline the mountains thrust up, snow still on their heads. One stood out. A man could imagine a great ear, its side turned up to listen.

Two sleeps to Fort Benton. Two sleeps and the better part of three days unless a man had a burr in his pants. More than once he had bought whiskey there and tobacco and horseshoes when they had them. And because he was randy he had laid up with squaws and felt shitty afterward, not just because he might catch a dose. What he needed was a woman like Teal Eye.

Three winters, one hard, they had passed on the Teton, with nothing to do but chop wood, kill meat and try to keep warm. For a man who wanted to be footloose, Summers sure had hobbled himself. Father to a boy more than two years old, guardian or something to a blind one, near-husband of Teal Eye. Once in a while still Higgins could see the far look in Summers' eyes, the look of things undone maybe, the look of other times, other places, ahead or behind. Who could tell?

When her time came on her, Teal Eye had ordered the men away, pointing low to the western sky for the hour of return. Summers had fumed but obeyed. When they got back, there was Teal Eye on her feet and a boy baby cozy under a blanket. Summers had watched it and watched it and one day came out of the tepee with a smile on his face and a choke in his voice. "Hig, he can see! My boy can see!"

So now here he was, one mateless Higgins, bound for the fort with a hell's list of things to buy and to do if he could. Trade in skins that Summers had gathered, buy supplies, buy horses if he could, and, of all the damn things, get a stand on a preacher if he could find one. Summers wanted to get married but not by a priest.

"I got nothin' against Catholics," he had said, "but it's not my religion."

Higgins had to grin. "Not mine either," he answered and went on, knowing he spoke for both of them. "No tellin' what is."

"I'll take what I know against what I don't."

He rode on through the spring day. It was all fresh — fresh sky, fresh earth, fresh growth. The sun was kind and the west wind pushed him along. A long-billed bird circled around him, crying alarm. An early nester, he guessed. A couple of prairie chickens flushed up from some bushes. Their chuckles might be those of a girl. To his left was a small bunch of buffalo. One had calved. The skyline waved ahead of him, unfixed and far off.

He camped and ate jerky that Teal Eye had fixed and had a pipe afterward and went to sleep counting the stars.

◣ ◣ ◣

It was late afternoon when he wound down a long slope and came in close sight of the fort. It rose there, gray, without windows, and might have housed dead people. Two blockhouses with loopholes rose above the walls and jutted out from them. The whole building, he knew from before, had been made of mud shaped into big bricks and then dried. It couldn't be burned down, that was for sure. Close by, beyond some trees, the river ran. On the far side, upstream, a bare bluff stood. A little dancing wind played with dust there. A few tepees were scattered around the fort, the homes, he reckoned, of fort loafers or sometime workers.

He rode by the fort and watered his string, then came back and tied the string to a tree. He unlashed the two bundles of furs he had brought. They were heavy but not beyond carrying.

A small door opened in the sally port, and the guard said, "Hiya there, Hig. How'd you winter?"

"Saved all my parts anyhow. Major in?"

"Yep. You know where."

He walked into a big yard with storehouses right and left and behind him. An Indian was dickering at one. At another two men were stacking buffalo hides. A clerk or some such was watching and counting. The hides made a stink.

The agent's quarters were in the rear. Higgins knocked and was told to come in.

Major Culbertson sat at a rough desk. Papers with figures on them lay on it. He got up and moved ahead to shake hands. "Welcome, Hig. Put those furs down." Culbertson was a large, friendly man with a mustache and beard and a high forehead. He had a look of good faith about him. "Glad to see you. Take a chair."

"Open for trade, Major?"

"That's what we're here for, but why be so sudden? Hard winter, you had?"

"We made it through. Had meat enough. You ask me what's hardest, campin' out way we do, and I would say keepin' clean."

"I can imagine, lice and all."

"No, sir. No lice in Teal Eye's camp. You can bet the whole fort on that."

"Go on."

"Hands, face, the whole hide, that's what's hard to keep clean. Without soap, I mean."

"It's not much of an item of trade with us. The staff uses it mostly. I think we can spare a few bars. It's harsh, you know."

"Not nigh as rough as sand."

Culbertson smiled. "How about a drink?"

"I wouldn't want to hurt your feelin's by refusin'."

Culbertson reached in his desk and got out a bottle. From a shelf he took two glasses. He didn't believe in dinky drinks. Sipping, he asked, "What all do you need, Hig?"

"I could leave the order with one of the men?"

"Nonsense. When you or Dick Summers come in, I want to see you. Now what do you need?"

"Tobacco and whiskey, first off."

The items went down on a piece of paper. "And?"

"Meal or flour if you have any. Dried beans, too. The quiet kind."

"I believe we have a few pounds of beans. I can't guarantee the silence."

"Put saleratus down, then."

"Saleratus? Lord, we're not exactly a grocery."

"A pinch or two in the pot quiets the beans down."

"Maybe we can find some."

"How about horseshoes?"

"I'll speak to the blacksmith."

"A couple of blankets. Teal Eye wants 'em. And some beads. She does purty beadwork."

"All that's not so much."

"I'm comin' to somethin' else. We need horses, good ones, four of 'em."

Culbertson looked at the furs on the floor and shook his head. "I'm afraid — "

"Not for them. Here." Higgins reached in his pocket, got out the two gold pieces Summers had given him and handed them over.

"Hum," Culbertson said. "It's enough, but you know our Indians attach no importance to gold. It has to be translated into goods."

"I figured that. Will you do it?"

"It will take time. Minimum two days. I must get in touch with some men that I trust. But, sure. I'll tackle it."

He poured another drink. "Now back to your order. What else?"

"I might think of somethin' while we wait."

"Good enough. Let's look at the furs."

"Beaver and mink."

Culbertson left his chair and stooped and, one by one, felt of the pelts. "Those were the days," he said as if speaking to himself. "Fine furs. Not coarse stuff. Not buffalo hides and tongues."

"Summers would as lief bring in his own skin as bring in a buffalo hide."

"Yes. Yes. These, you know, aren't worth what they were, but they'll more than cover your order. You'll have something coming back."

"Make it credit. And, hey, before I forget it, how about scissors? "

Culbertson smiled. "Scissors, too?"

"Handier than a knife sometimes."

Culbertson returned to his chair and asked after a swallow, "How is Summers?"

"Same as usual. Damn good man."

"No doubt about that."

"He still wants to get married. He's set on it."

"I ought to know. Every time he's here, maybe half a dozen times altogether, he badgers me about it, as if I could produce a preacher out of thin air. Too bad he won't have a priest."

Culbertson sipped at his whiskey and smiled, looking satisfied as he spoke. "This time I just may be able to oblige him."

"You got a preacher in stock?"

"We don't deal in that kind of cloth, but it happens there's a minister here. Methodist. He's out exploring or teaching the Gospel right now. I'm expecting him for dinner."

"Will you make it so's I can talk to him?"

"Easy. You'll eat with us, too. There'll just be four, you, the minister, Major Dawson and I. My wife and the children are visiting her people, the weather being nice for a change."

"Dick'll thank you. So do I."

"Fine. Now where are your horses?"

"Tied to a tree outside."

"Turn them into the corral. Safer that way. We have a little feed left."

╲ ╲ ╲

Higgins tended to the horses. He bought a towel and a comb on credit and then, seeing no washstand, went down to the river where he washed hands and face and combed his hair. The river ran clear, as it wouldn't when the rains came. It was time to chop off some of his hair.

He looked at the sun, almost out of sight behind the big hill. Time for supper? He didn't want to be early or want to be late. He asked the guard at the door when the major's suppertime was.

"About now," the man told him.

Two men were in the office with Culbertson. Culbertson waved a hand and said, "Good timing, Hig. I want you to meet Brother Potter and Major Dawson. Gentlemen, Mr. Higgins."

The one he called brother stepped forward, saying, "Bless you. Brother Culbertson has told us about you." His hand was big and solid. He was a stocky man, not quite fat, with a bald head and a long coat, which told the world he was a preacher.

Major Dawson smiled as he held out his hand. He was thinner than the other two and looked more used to the weather. Shaved smooth, his face was a little pinched up between nose and chin as if he found things to laugh at.

"Major Dawson is the actual agent here, I'm so often away," Culbertson said. "Business in St. Louis and elsewhere."

Dawson shook his head, a small smile on his lips. "The de facto factor just in his absence."

The men were all dressed in town clothes — cloth coats, cloth pants, cloth vests, neckties. No place for buckskins, Higgins thought. No place for worn and soiled leather. But what the hell?

Culbertson opened a door and said, "Dinner is ready."

There was a table in the room with a white cloth on it. There were knives and forks, spoons and glasses. Culbertson asked them to be seated, showing them where. A woman came in with a bottle. A part-blood, she wore a skirt and a blouse. "A little wine for thy stomach's sake, Reverend?" Culbertson asked as the woman started to pour.

"How can I refuse when the words are in the book? But first, brothers, please, the blessing."

He had a passel of things to say to the Lord before he came to amen.

The woman brought in a hump roast on a platter. Next time in, she carried a big bowl of hominy and a saucer of sliced onions in vinegar.

"The Lord's bounty," Potter said, eyeing the food. "His infinite bounty."

"It will be more bounteous when the boats start arriving," Culbertson said while he carved. "Meat and hominy, that's standard winter fare. And this is the last of the onions."

"There'll be a slew of 'em growin' wild in two-three weeks," Higgins said, just to be part of the talk.

Dawson smiled at him, nodding. "Right."

"I suppose you live mostly on straight meat?" Culbertson asked Higgins.

"Only kind of. Summers' woman knows a lot about wild stuff, roots and leaves and berries and such. We live pretty good."

Potter swallowed a mouthful of meat, chased it with a drink of water and said, "The man's wife, you mean?"

"Well —"

Culbertson came to his rescue. "You pitch us into a subject I had thought to talk about later. Perhaps it's just as well. The man, Dick Summers, I count with our better men."

Higgins said, "Count higher."

Culbertson smiled and went on. "For a number of years he has lived with an Indian woman. They have a child now. He wants to be married, but not by a priest."

Potter said, "I see."

"Pity you're not a Presbyterian," Dawson put in.

"Let not us Protestants quarrel," Potter told him. "I wouldn't say the same of the Papists." He went back to his plate.

"To go on," Culbertson said, "it would take most of a week for Summers and his family to get here. Can you wait, Brother Potter?"

Potter passed his plate for more meat. He chewed and thought. "I could perform the ceremony there."

Higgins took a long breath. "It's a long ways. I been makin' cold camps."

"I wouldn't advise it," Dawson told him.

"I would go in the hands of the Lord and fear not."

Culbertson put his folded hands on the table. "You wouldn't have to be afraid of our Blackfeet with Higgins leading you. He is by way of becoming a legend. May I tell him, Hig?"

"If you want to."

"The Blackfeet call Higgins Broken Mouth, the Friend of the Great Bear. And his friend, Summers, he is the Bear Maker. Come a pinch, he can summon the white bear out of the ground, out of the air, out of nowhere, but there it will be."

Higgins said, "That was a long while ago."

"That's why it's a legend. Tell how it all came about, Hig."

"Summers does better."

"Belief in miracles is not restricted to us," Dawson said, not as if it mattered.

"Go ahead, Hig."

So he told them about Old Ephraim and the meeting with the Blackfeet and Old Ephraim towering up just in time.

Potter had cleaned his plate. He leaned back and told them, "I must meet this man Summers."

"You won't be disappointed," Culbertson said. "Say, Hig, what's his interest in a killing that occurred four or six years ago?"

"You got me."

"It seems that two men friends, white, coveted the same Blackfoot girl. Or maybe one just suspected the other of playing him false with the woman. It didn't happen near here, and the truth is hard to come by. Anyhow, the one man killed the other and took off, never to be seen again hereabouts."

"And the woman?" Higgins asked.

"All I know is she wouldn't stay with the tribe."

Higgins let out "Ah-h" without meaning to. Culbertson regarded him with curiosity, but Potter broke in. "Yes, I must meet this man, if Brother Higgins will take me to him." His eyes asked the question.

Higgins shied at the idea. Towing a saddle-sore preacher over the miles? Listening to the talk-talk about the good Lord? He wouldn't be in the hands of the Lord. He would be in the hands of Higgins, who was a long shot from grace. But Preacher Potter was so oncoming. And Summers did want to be married. He said, "I guess all right."

"Probably day after tomorrow," Culbertson said. "I believe I can have your horses by then, Hig."

Higgins lingered after Potter and Dawson had gone. "I been thinkin', Major. You know, our manners ain't high class. Horn spoons and a common pot to eat out of."

"I've done the same."

"But this with the preacher is special. In our order could you throw in some spare tin stuff, like knives, forks and spoons and maybe cups?"

"I'll do it, Hig."

"And some red cloth for Teal Eye?"

Culbertson put a hand on his arm. "All that will be my gift. Good night, Hig."

16

Higgins looked over the four horses Culbertson had bargained for. They were on the small side, as Indian stock usually was. From their teeth he judged that the oldest was about eight, a good useful age. One of them, the one that caught the eye, wasn't quite to his liking. It was a pinto, and to his way of thinking a solid color meant a solider horse. They were all a mite skittish.

They were gathered outside the fort, he and Potter and Culbertson and half a dozen Indian men who stood watching off to one side.

Culbertson asked, "Satisfied, Hig? They were the best I could do on short notice."

"Thanks. Plumb pleased." The horses ought to be shod, but he had given up that idea. They had never known a shoe and wouldn't take kindly to having any tacked on. On each of them he would have had to use a rope and pull up a leg and anchor it, raised, to the horse's neck. No thanks. Not now. Anyhow, the way ahead wasn't too rocky.

The broken pack horses were ready. He had put the untried ones between the older horses. They weren't carrying anything and should lead along all right. He shied a look at Potter. The man had on his long coat and wore a hat with a small brim and a domed, undented crown. He would find soon enough how the wind liked it.

Right now the air was still, and a glow in the east, above the far, deep-sloping bank of the Missouri, showed the sun would be peeking up soon.

He set to work bridling and saddling the new horse that looked gentlest. Against emergencies he would have to lead away with the trained horse he had ridden in. This new one was for Potter. Culbertson had gone over to the hitch rack and came back leading the pack string.

"Ready?" Higgins asked Potter.

"Don't worry about me, Brother. I have ridden before."

"We head west. Up the hill and due west."

Higgins helped Potter get his considerable bulk in the saddle and handed him the reins.

The horse got its head down, crow-hopped and jumped, its back arched like a bow. Potter's hat sailed off first, spooking the string. Potter followed it and hit the ground with a bump.

Potter didn't need Higgins' outstretched hand or answer the question, "You hurt?" He got up, smiling, and said, "A lesson in humility."

The Indian men were bent over, laughing.

Potter went on, " 'Blessed be the meek, for they shall inherit the earth.' " He rubbed his right ham. "It was a rough introduction to inheritance, if any." He still wore his big smile. "The earth hereabouts has no give to it."

Culbertson had caught up the saddle horse. The pack string

had quieted. Higgins said, pointing, "Maybe you'd better try that horse."

"No, Brother Higgins. No, indeed. If I am taught to be humble, I am taught to have faith."

"And hang on to your hat."

Potter regarded the stiff hat on the ground. "Without it I'll sunburn." He ran a hand over his bald head.

"I got somethin' might do," Higgins said. "Might do if you don't mind sweatin' some." He dug from a pack his old coonskin cap, which he had brought along just in case. Potter put it on. "Thank you, Brother Higgins. I shall not complain of its warmth." Higgins put the stiff hat in a pack, denting it some.

Potter mounted his horse again without hesitation, saying as he put his foot in a stirrup, "Be good, Dobbin, or invite the Lord's wrath." The horse snorted, took a couple of steps and stood still.

Higgins swung up on his own horse. Culbertson handed the lead rope of the string to him, then offered his hand. He shook hands with Potter, too, who said, "Thank you, Brother Culbertson. I shall return the saddle you've loaned me. The Lord loves you."

Spring on the plains was a high old time, Higgins thought after they had climbed out of the valley. Wildflowers starting up. Grass greening. Birds mating. The songs of meadowlarks sounding. Gophers standing like soldiers, then diving into their holes with flirts of their tails. Jack rabbits bounding from bushes, then sitting straight, their ears up. It was the time of new things, of old things born again.

Midmorning now and the sun high, not burning, and the sky like a still lake, upside down, its shores the far skylines. Laze along, horse. Just laze along.

A jack rabbit bounded up, almost under the feet of Potter's horse, and the horse shied and reared and set off on a high lope.

Potter's butt bounced in the saddle. He clutched the saddle horn with both hands. His long coat, unbuttoned, flapped out at the sides. He was a big bat, hanging hard to a horse.

Higgins kicked his horse and yanked at the string. He couldn't leave the pack horses, not with untried ones in the string. He kicked and yanked again. Potter, still more or less in his seat, disappeared over a swell of land.

It took a while to catch up with him. The horse stood quiet and spent, its belly heaving, its sweat drying. Potter was still in the saddle.

You couldn't scare that man or make him mad, Higgins thought, seeing the big smile.

"A spirited ride," Potter said. "One I'll remember."

"You stuck the horse."

"By a miracle."

"And kept him pointed west to boot."

"I fear I had nothing to do with that. Thank the horse. Shall we proceed?"

"If you're ready."

A thunder shower came up before they made camp, a warm shower that was more noise and flash than rain. It passed over, and they reached a small gulch that ran with water, and here Higgins decided to make camp.

Potter got off his horse stiffly and held on to the saddle horn long enough to get his legs under him.

Higgins asked, "Stove up?"

"A little sore in the knees, a little galled where I sit, but nothing more than that. It was a grand day."

He looked to the west, and Higgins followed his gaze. Low clouds were banked there, slow-moving, on fire, and the fire blazed up and touched off higher clouds, and against the flames a lone eagle soared. Potter murmured, "Majestic," and bent his head.

Higgins turned away. He led the horses to water and put the new ones on picket, driving the picket pins deep. He unloaded the two old pack horses.

While he was doing that, Potter asked, "Where are the buffalo, Brother Higgins?"

"Most of 'em's down south, I reckon. They'll be showin' up. There's some that stay the year round. You'll see 'em.

"I don't aim to make a fire," Higgins told Potter, who had taken a seat on a piece of dry canvas. "Just a small fire inside, I'm thinkin' on. Is a drink against your religion?"

"Some would say so. Not I. The love of the Lord should be a joyous thing, not a long list of 'don'ts.' Bring the jug, Brother Higgins."

Potter knew how to drink out of it.

They ate cold buffalo roast that Culbertson had insisted they take.

Afterward, smoking, Higgins asked, "Just what brung you here, Brother Potter?" He wanted to say Preacher Potter, it sounded so good to the ear.

"Why, the wish to save souls."

"Ain't there lost souls everywhere?"

"Yes, but the Lord called me here. Called me to minister to the untutored children of nature."

"Meanin' Injuns?"

"To be sure."

"They got their own religion, I hear tell."

"Not the true, saving religion. Not the love of Jesus."

"Savin'. Savin' from what?"

"The fires of hell, of course."

"They been here a long time, the Injuns. You think the dead ones that never had a chance to know Jesus, you think they're in hell?"

Potter shook his head slowly and put a hand to it. "Brother Higgins, who knows the way of the Lord? I can't answer your question. What we can be sure of is that all of God's judgments, all his manifestations, are right and true, no matter that we often can't comprehend them. Of one thing I am certain. Those who have been introduced to Jesus and love him not are doomed. Are you a believer, Brother Higgins?"

"In some things. In quite a bunch of things."

"Look about you. Everywhere is plenty. The beasts of the

fields, the birds of the air, all put there for man, for his food or his delight. Look at the soil that grows food for us. Look at the skies that give us sunshine and rain. It is all God's bounty, his gifts to mankind."

"I don't see much use in gnats and rattlesnakes."

"Ah, to test us. To make sure that our love and faith don't falter under adversity."

"I ain't of a mind to argue much, but it sounds wrong for true love to be so tormented."

"The Lord knows best. Be sure of that."

Potter got up stiffly and put a hand on Higgins' shoulder. "You are a good man, Brother Higgins. You will come to see. I pray that you will. Now, if you'll excuse me, I'll say my prayers and go to bed."

Higgins smoked for a while longer. So everything was made for man, was it? Seemed like the other critters ought to have a vote in the final say. They were here, and along comes Mr. High and Mighty Man and says you're all mine. You were made just for me. Talk about being meek.

What would Dick Summers say to that? He'd probably grin and answer, "Every man to his own way of thinkin'. You can't change that. Just remember, Hig, says I who has no right to say it, frettin' your mind binds your bowels."

17

HIGGINS' horse wanted to drink, but he curbed it and kicked it and splashed across the stream, dragging the string along with him. He put a hand over his eyes against the slanting sun and yelled, "Hey, Dick. Company."

Summers came from behind his tepee, an ax in his hand. "You caught me onexpected," he said, but Higgins knew that he hadn't. Summers was too keen to be caught.

Higgins turned. "Come across, Brother Potter. Your horse can drink later. Come on."

Potter came on. The spray of water under hoof blinked like crystal in the long light.

Higgins grinned down at Summers. "I reckon I done pretty good, Dick."

Potter almost fell as his feet touched the ground. He hobbled over, his hand out. "Brother Summers, isn't it?"

Higgins had to laugh, but didn't, at Summers' face. The preacher went on, "I am Brother Potter of the Methodist Episcopal Church."

Summers got out, "Welcome. Long way from home."

"Not really, Brother. Not at all. Not where I'm welcome."

Teal Eye came out of the tepee. Summers waved her to come on, and she did, acting bashful. Summers said, "This is Teal Eye."

Potter held out his hand. "Bless you, Sister."

She touched his hand and turned to the fire and the pot over it. The two boys weren't in sight. It was likely they were hiding, being bashful, too. One thing for sure: they were together.

"I hope you like the four nags I bought," Higgins said. "We got a credit at the fort."

"They look passin' good. What say we unpack? No, no, Mr. Potter. You just set on that log there and rest yourself."

They left him sitting and stepped to the horses. As they fiddled with ropes, Higgins spoke softly. "Dick, I tuck it on myself to get knives and forks and them things. All tin, of course. Special occasion, seemed to me." He looked at Summers, a question in his eyes.

A smile touched Summers' mouth. "You shine, Hig. You shine for a fact. I can tell Teal Eye just what to do, me bein' high born."

"Culbertson, he threw in some beads and red cloth, present for Teal Eye."

They got the horses unpacked and the goods stowed away. Higgins said, "I'd best hobble or picket the new horses."

"I aim to do that. You look some fagged, I'm thinkin', and I want to look over the stock you bought. So far, so good, seems like."

"Dick, the preacher don't object to a snort."

Summers nodded and led away.

At the fire Potter said to Higgins, "This is a smiling valley, Brother. A man forgets his aches and pains."

Higgins cast his eye around. The ripples of the river ran red,

catching the beams of a sun soon to set. Eastward the valley
flowed yellow and warm until the far banks rose to benchlands.
The mountains were darkening, black purple as the sun slid behind them. For once no wind blew, not even a breeze, and the
campfire smoke lifted lazy and straight. A fish jumped in the
stream.

"Glad you like it," Higgins was saying. "It ain't too bad a
place for a fact."

"What do you suppose — I mean at what hour Brother Summers might prefer for the ceremony?"

"It's his to say, I reckon."

"Of course. For myself, I suggest sunrise, the beginning of a
new day, of a new way."

"Suits me all right. I ain't one to lie abed."

Near them, Teal Eye stirred the pot and added some sticks
to the fire. The two boys were staying out of sight even now.
Summers came back and said, "Them new horses ain't bad."

Potter cleared his throat. "Brother Summers, I hope I'm not
mistaken, you do want to be married?"

Summers looked him in the face. "Have for a long time. Been
waitin' to find me a preacher, that I have."

"Fine. What time, Brother? I have suggested sunrise."

"Whenever you say. We'll be ready." Summers walked off,
beckoning to Teal Eye. Likely he wanted to tell her about high-
born manners. When he came back, he brought buffalo robes
and spread them on the ground.

Potter said, "These old bones of mine can't get used to sitting
as you men and the Indians do. What is it called? Yes, a tailor's
squat."

"You set right on that log," Summers told him. "I got somethin' might ease your miseries."

That was the signal for Higgins to get up and fetch the jug.

"We're froze for glasses," Summers said, meaning they didn't
have any.

"He" — Higgins pointed — "knows how to drink from a jug.
Done it before."

Summers uncorked the jug and handed it to Potter. Potter put a forefinger in the handle, rested the jug on his elbow, put his mouth to the opening and lifted the elbow.

Summers' teeth showed in a grin. "Reverend, you been places."

"That I have. And seen things and drunk worse spirits than this." He passed the jug.

They had one drink each. Then Summers rose, saying, "Nigh time to eat."

With a horn spoon Teal Eye ladled food into a tin cup. Summers took it, put it on a tin plate and added knife, fork and spoon. He handed the plate to Potter. He did the same then for Higgins and himself. Teal Eye tended to her own.

Higgins felt laughter in him and held it back. For God's sake, Summers, that old mountain-man son of a bitch, playing waiter and being dainty about it!

"Please, let me ask the blessing before we eat," Potter said. The blessing was full of thanks and didn't ask much. He was, Higgins thought, a man satisfied with what had been given. That wasn't a bad way to be.

Potter took a spoonful of stew, rolled it around, chewed and swallowed. He raised his eyes high and then looked at Teal Eye. "What a tasty dish! What flavoring! What's your secret, Sister?"

Teal Eye looked at Summers who answered for her. "She knows a sight of things, wild things to eat, like roots of cattails and balsamroot and stuff you wouldn't think. Main thing is good buffalo meat."

"Indians have to know," Teal Eye said. "Know or go dead." Those were almost her first words to the preacher. The shyness was wearing off.

"Far better than fort victuals. Tell me, where are the boys? Two of them, aren't there?"

"You'll see 'em in time," Summers answered. "They're small and wary as animals, not used to seein' anybody but us."

As if acting on the words, Teal Eye rose, filled two more cups and took them inside the tepee.

Their meal finished, they sat back. Potter patted his stomach. Higgins and Summers lighted pipes.

"Crack of dawn, you say?" Summers asked.

"Sunup, yes." With his hand Potter kept congratulating his stomach. "A new day. Did you ever pause to think every morning was a new beginning?"

"And every night, you're glad to be rid of that day, huh?" Higgins asked just for the hell of it.

Summers said, "Please to quit that pickin', Hig."

"Every night, thanks, I would hope. Goodbye to a day well spent."

The sun had sunk long since, but the sky was still filled with afterglow. Overhead was the sound of a wing.

Potter yawned. "Speaking of sleep — "

Higgins told him, "You can crawl into my tepee. I'd as soon sleep outside."

"No, Brother Higgins. I have my own bedroll, and I like to sleep under the stars."

"Your choice. I'll get your roll."

"If you would. I confess to a certain stiffness of limb."

They saw Potter bedded down on a robe. The fire was dead. Teal Eye had disappeared. Pretty soon Potter began snoring, snoring in praise of the Lord maybe.

Higgins was tired himself and so said good night and went to his tepee.

* * *

Teal Eye sat on a robe inside the tepee, waiting for Summers. The boys were asleep. Before bedtime Summers liked to step away from the camp, look at the stars, sniff the air and listen to the sounds of the night.

She told herself not to be moody. A woman ought to be cheerful with her man, cheerful and helpful, not anxious, not worried. But here, tomorrow, came the day of a proper, white-man marriage, and she drew in on herself. Before now Summers had talked of a preacher and a wedding, more often since she had borne him a baby, but she had shied away from his words, saying inside herself that the time never would come.

She could stand up with Summers and be married, but there would be darkness in her, the weight of a truth untold. Maybe better to speak straight with her man even if it meant losing him. Maybe tell all and go on without him. She wouldn't let herself cry.

Summers came in the tepee and waited until he could see in the darkness. Then he said, "Still up, girl? Worried about the big day?"

"Me feel — I feel — we must make talk. Not here. By the river."

He said, "Sure," and came and helped lift her up and walked with her past the sleeping camp to the river bank. They sat down. He said, "Tell me."

She didn't know where to begin or whether she could carry through to the end. She tried, "You want true woman?"

"Got one. Don't need another."

"Not so."

"You keepin' something terrible from me, huh?"

In the starshine she could see his face. It was a kind, strong face. She didn't want to put hurt in it. She turned her eyes.

"Maybe better not tell." The words came out low.

"Maybe better tell, but I won't push you. Won't make any difference. We stay together."

His voice, she thought, was as untroubled as the little water by the shore. It helped her to go on.

"Boone Caudill — " she hated to say the name — "he killed Jim Deakins."

"I knowed that from before."

It seemed to her that she had to take her strength in both hands, to squeeze her heart to her throat. "It was — it was — it was over me. Boone Caudill's woman once. Me."

To her surprise he said, "I kind of figured that out."

"He was your friend, yes? Caudill?"

"Onct. Just onct." He shook his head. "That dumb bastard." His hand tightened on her arm. "I aim to see him sometime."

"No. No. It is all over."

"All over for Jim Deakins. That's a fact." His voice was hard and the hand still tight on her arm.

"Please, no. I ask please. Not to see him. Not to think."

"Ease off, girl. Sometime. Just maybe sometime. Let's not fret ourselves." His hand loosened and patted the arm it had squeezed. "Now about you? What's the trouble?"

"I be so afraid."

"Afraid? Of what?"

"I tell you the truth, and maybe you no want to marry me."

He laughed a low laugh, and his voice was gentle. "Think I could change my mind? Think I'm crazy? Only thing I'm crazy about is you." He leaned over and kissed her under the ear.

The worst was over. She could go on. "Baby born with red hair. Jim Deakins have red hair. So Boone shoot him. But it is not so. It is not true. Me not lie with Jim Deakins. Baby belong Boone."

"Sure. The looks of him say so."

"Then Boone leave me. I want no man. I fight. I sneak away from camp. No man until you."

He put his arm across her shoulders. Into her hair he said, "For Christ's sake! To be afraid! When all the time I'm set on marryin' you. And we'll give Nocansee a name. Not, by God, Caudill. It's Summers he'll be. Now how are you, Mrs. Summers? How's my little duck?"

Against his chest she tried not to cry but cried just the same. "You be so good. You forget Boone? Yes?"

"If I can. If I can. He ain't our worry." His free hand found and held her breast. "Since we're about to get married, I got me an idee."

She lifted her face, knowing it was tear-stained, and met his eyes and was able to smile. She said, "Good."

18

THE CAMP stirred before the sun came up. Low in the east, Higgins saw, a bank of clouds lay red, catching the upcoming light. Potter might have been first out of bed. He had on another long coat, clean but wrinkled, a white shirt and a tie. From his log he waved a greeting and turned back, facing east, his big hands folded over a book. Higgins could hear Summers and Teal Eye rustling around in their tepee.

Then Teal Eye came out. She had tied a red sash around clean buckskins and wore red bows on her braids. The sash showed how slender she was, how slender and well put together. Higgins searched for words to describe her. "Comely" came to mind. So did a stranger word, "winsome." But they weren't enough, singly or together. How describe the honest, warm spirit in her eyes?

Potter said, "Good morning, Sister," and got to his feet. "A glorious day."

Summers had new buckskins on, not a fringe lost or tattered. He looked too young and strong for gray hair.

Potter greeted him and said, "The day shines on us."

The sun hadn't appeared yet, but all the eastern sky told of its coming.

Summers smiled and said, "I reckon we're ready."

"Fine. Fine. So am I."

Potter had them stand together, facing east. Higgins took a place off to one side.

With his book in his hand, the preacher cleared his throat, bowed his head and said, "Let us pray."

It wasn't like Summers to bow his head, but he did, maybe so as not to hurt Potter's feelings. Teal Eye copied him.

Potter's full voice rose, sounding over the cawing of a couple of magpies upstream. For a flash Higgins wondered how many ears God had. A heap of them to hear all the prayers. Nocansee and the boy had crept to the flap of the big tepee. They sat shy, holding hands.

The preacher read from the book. "Dearly beloved, we are gathered together here in the sight of God —"

Summers and Teal Eye stood close together, their faces lifted. A good-matched couple, Higgins thought, better matched than any he had ever known. Summers had said he didn't want his boy to be a bastard. That was the why of the marriage. But it was more than that. Something in Summers wanted him and Teal Eye to be bound, tied together in law so as to be able to look any man in the face and say, "This is my wife."

Potter was reading, "I require and charge you both —"

Here a man ought to pay close attention in order to know what he was letting himself in for if ever he married.

The first of the sun's rays was shining on them now, lighting Summers' gray eyes and Teal Eye's dark ones, bringing out the silver on the edges of Potter's bald head. He stood square and solid, the preacher did, doing what was solemn to him. And it came to Higgins that it was solemn, maybe sacred, and the stray thoughts in him hushed up, and he lowered his head and listened.

"Wilt thou take this woman to be thy wedded wife, to live together after God's ordinance in the holy state of matrimony? Wilt thou love her, comfort her, honor and keep her, in sickness and in health and, forsaking all others, keep thee only unto her, so long as ye both shall live?"

Summers' "I will" came out strong and clear.

Potter asked the same things of Teal Eye. For an answer she took Summers' hand and said, "My man."

There was some more reading then, ending with "Our Father who art in heaven —" Higgins had known all the words once.

The preacher, beaming, shook hands with them both, said something about signing a paper with Higgins as witness and went on. "Now, Brother Summers, do you want the boys baptized? I think I see them both watching."

Summers looked at Teal Eye but seemed to find no answer there. Of a sudden he grinned and said, "Might as well go the whole way, I reckon."

"Fine. Fine. Some water then." Potter walked toward the tepee.

Nocansee sat with his head bowed, the little boy between his knees. Potter said to the little one, "Can you speak your name, my son?"

Summers answered for him. "It's Lije, short for Elijah."

"A good biblical name." Potter sprinkled water on the boy's head. "Elijah Summers, I baptize thee in the name of the Father, the Son and the Holy Spirit."

Potter said then to Nocansee, "Your turn, my son. What is your name?"

His face still lowered, the boy answered, "Nocansee."

Potter didn't catch on. "Nocansee Summers, I baptize thee in the name of the Father, the Son and the Holy Spirit."

He wiped his wet fingers on his pants. "Now, son, look up, look up. It is a glad day." He put a hand on the boy's head and tilted it up, and words died in his throat. He put a gentle hand on Nocansee's shoulder and turned away, saying to himself, "The Lord knows best." He shook his head as if to get rid of doubt.

Higgins saw tears on his cheeks.

19

THE SUN was just winking up through the mists that shimmered on the far skyline. Looking back, Summers could see the tops of the mountains, colored pink above the darkness below. Ahead the plains spread, showing a growing green. Beside him rode Potter and Higgins and behind him plodded the two pack horses he led.

They rode in silence, but his ears remembered what Potter had said. "Will I strain your hospitality if I remain for a day or two?"

He wouldn't. Not much, though Summers felt an itch in his gizzard, an itch to be going places, known and unknown, to see men he had partnered with, including one man in particular. What would he do, what could he do, when he caught up with Boone Caudill? Just pass the time of day and shake hands?

That didn't fill the bill. By rights a man ought to have to pay in some kind of measure for what he did wrong. He ought at least to look his past in the eye.

Anyhow, here was the preacher, a big and friendly and out-going man, no matter if God kept coming into his talk. He was almighty curious about what a man believed, but his questions didn't rub up a sore. They were kind-meant, and he didn't argue over the answers.

He had wanted to go on a buffalo hunt, saying, "I have a picture of myself, riding boldly among the fleeing beasts, bow and arrow in hand." He gave his big grin then. "Boyish, I know. I should put away childish things."

Summers had answered, "I reckon we all make up pictures, and no harm in it. Wisht I could oblige you, Parson — "

"Brother, please."

"Wisht I could oblige you, Brother Potter, but of buffalo horses we got none. More'n that, we don't want to run the buffalo to hell — pardon me — out of reach. Too scarce this time of year."

"What do we do?"

"Still hunt. Get a stand on a bunch and take our pick."

Summers slowed down his saddle horse. "Seein' you ride," he said, "it come to me you must be almighty saddle-sore."

"A minor affliction." Potter made a sweep with his hand. "How can it trouble me on this, God's good morning?"

The sun had cleared the mists. The meadowlarks were singing. Gophers stood straight, dived for their holes, turned around and peeked up. A curlew circled them, crying. Wild flags were coming up. Plant and animal, Summers thought, had come alive with the soil's warming. A soft wind blew out of the west.

He brought the party to a halt while his eyes searched the land. Potter used this time to ask, "Where do you place your trust, Brother Summers?"

"There was buffalo hereabouts not long ago."

"That ain't what he asked," Higgins put in with a wink.

"Oh, trust. Seems like I've had to put it in myself mostly." He smiled at Potter. "Not sayin' it ain't sometimes hard to do."

"That's a sound answer insofar as it goes. Jesus was a resolute man. We think of Him as meek, but when the occasion arose He was resolute, and we shouldn't forget it."

Summers spoke to his horse, and they got under way. To their left two coyotes limped along out of range. Winter skinny, they had learned the way of men and of guns. They had learned, too, that hunters left something behind them.

Summers said a soft "Whoa." They had mounted a slope, and, looking down, saw buffalo grazing. They hadn't taken alarm, though closer than Summers would have liked while on horseback. "Time to sneak up," he said, sliding from his horse.

"They aren't very many," Potter said.

"A little early yet. Week or so and you'll see nothin' but humps. Give a few years, and it could be you'll see nothin' but bones." He stooped and went forward, setting the example.

Behind him Potter whispered, "But the horses?"

"Old ones. They'll stay around."

As they drew closer, Summers went to his belly. He crawled a piece and examined his Hawken. It was ready to shoot as he knew it would be, but a careful man always made sure.

Potter had crawled up beside him. He put out an asking hand. "Could you — would you allow — ?"

"Sure thing," Summers answered. "See that young cow, third from the left. Aim at her. But wait!"

He pulled the ramrod from the rifle, planted it upright ahead of him, held it with his left hand and laid the barrel over his extended arm. "Best shoot from a rest. This way. See?"

Potter did as told.

"Aim behind the shoulder, some lower than you might think the heart is. Then fire away."

Potter was a long time lining up the sights. He stopped for a minute so's to get a tighter hold on the ramrod. Too tight, Summers knew. It made his arm tremble.

At last he fired. The bullet went high, puffing up dust on a ridge beyond his target.

Higgins said, "Reverend, I'm afeard you just potted an angel."

Potter eased his body over to one side. It shook as he said, "You can't take me in, Mr. Sheriff." Between chuckles he went on, "It can't be murder. Angels are immortal."

"Want to try again?" Summers asked, recharging the Hawken.

"No. No. We came to make meat. They're moving off."

Without using a rest, Summers lifted the rifle and fired. The cow humped over and fell.

Potter said, "You didn't even have time to aim."

"He just points and lets go," Higgins put in.

"It's an art, an act of genius."

Summers said, "Practice."

They butchered out the cow, brought up the horses and loaded.

On the way home Potter said, "The good Lord provides."

"Yep," Higgins said. "Him and good old Dick Summers."

▪ ▪ ▪

As they drew nearer the mountains, Potter pulled up his horse and said, " 'I lift up mine eyes . . .' "

Summers let him look. The highest mountain was maybe four miles away. It was also the nearest. It rose purple in the morning light, purple and white where snow draped it.

He had mounted Potter on Feather and would give him a gentle horse by way of a fee when he took off. Higgins had stayed behind, saying he would see could he catch him some trout. The weather was fair, with enough breeze in it to tickle the branches of scrub pine.

Potter asked, "What is the name of that noble height, Brother Summers?"

"They call it Elephant Ear Butte, but it's not a butte. I never seen an elephant."

"An unworthy name. I suggest Everlasting or, better yet, Soul Summit. Does it not refresh your soul?"

"I like to look at it."

Potter looked at it some more, his eyes wide and his mouth moving, no doubt to a prayer. He cut a funny figure with his preacher's coat and coonskin cap. He looked down, studying the ground, and lifted his leg over the cantle and dismounted with a grunt of satisfaction.

"The flowers," he said, examining one. "The lilies of the field."

"Lilies?"

"A figure. A manner of speaking." He plucked a bloom. "God is inventive. Look! Such a lovely, pale purple. What name, Brother Summers?"

"All I ever heard was windflowers. They come way early, first up you could say." Summers got off his horse.

"I do believe," Potter went on, "that it belongs to the buttercup family."

"It's strayed a piece, then. You studied flowers, Brother Potter?"

"Once I thought to be a botanist. That was before I heard the call." He dropped the flower he held and moved a step or two. "These tiny, red-purple blossoms, something like moss?"

"We call all the little, short stuff carpet flowers."

"The Lord spreads a carpet before us."

Summers looked at him and, like him, looked at the brave, frail first flowers, and it seemed to him his eyes had sharpened all at once. He had seen these things before, had seen and not seen, being concerned with bigger subjects, and now suddenly here were color and shape that he had passed by because they were tiny. He said, "Purty."

Potter gestured toward the mountain and then down at the ground. "The big and the little. The mighty and the minute. Can you doubt the power and the love of the Lord?"

"He's sure enough powerful."

They squatted on the turf. Summers picked a dry grass stem

and nibbled on it. "I worship a glad Lord," Potter told him. "We have set our faces against sin, as indeed we must, but in doing it I fear we have lost sight of joy. Joy, Brother Summers, delight in what we are given. Often I think God wants us not only to be good but to be radiant. Let us sing to the Lord."

"I don't know the tune."

A big, answering smile came on Potter's big face. "Another figure of speech. Let us sing in our hearts."

Potter squatted there, singing his song, Summers supposed. The world could stand preachers like him. He raised his gaze. "You have opened your doors to me, Brother. I was a stranger, and you took me in."

"We're beholden to you."

"Not at all. Not at all."

"It's little enough we got to give for what you done."

"Don't think that way. We are not in the marketplace. We give because we want to."

"Yes." Summers picked another blade of grass.

"The marketplace, the commerce, the financial intercourse of men, even perhaps the money-changers — these things are necessary, some of them, and not without worth. For myself, I rejoice in the open, free life. I dislike money unless it be employed for God's purposes. If I had money, I would establish a mission, a school, and teach the everyday arts as well as the love of Jesus. As it is, I am a traveling missionary with enough support to supply my few wants. What do you want that money can provide? Tell me that."

"Just a little tobacco and a jug once in a while. That's all Higgins wants, plus a wife."

"He wants one, then?"

"Needs one."

"What's holding him back?"

"Us, I guess. Me, maybe. We're so close, all of us, that he won't take off and look for himself."

"I see. Any other matter on your mind, Brother?"

"Not much. I'll just live off the land, long as I can, that is."

"But you're worried?"

"Not by you, Brother Potter. By what I see comin'. Men and more men, and the end of what I prize."

Potter put a hand to his jaw. "Go forth and multiply, the Bible says."

"And crowd the land." Summers had to smile, thinking. He turned to Potter. "You don't seem to be doin' so smart in the multiply department?"

Potter took time to laugh before saying, "Well taken, Brother. Maybe the Lord will forgive me." He sobered quickly. "But I understand what you're saying. The finish of a period. The termination of the kind of life you enjoy. I see it, too, and try to accept. All things come to an end. All things yield before new beginnings. Meantime, I put my faith in the Lord, who knows best."

"And live while we can."

"And live while we can — for the hereafter."

20

T HE WIND came, wind that charged down from the mountains, wave on wave, and tore down the slopes and battered the tepees, wind with the bite of last winter in it. Summers could hear the gusts coming. First there was a sound like low thunder, or buffalo on stampede, then came the whistling shrieks and then the fierce blow.

The trees and the underbrush slanted, and limbs flew, and the waters of the Teton whipped white, giving part of their spray to torn air.

He went outside, bending low, and found ropes and ran them around the crowns of the tepees and tied them to stout trees. Inside, the smoke whirled, blown away from the smoke hole, and reddened eyes leaked water. To be understood, he and Teal Eye and the boys had to raise their voices, sounding frail against the voice of the wind.

Teal Eye said, "Higgins, he will be coming back. He will fight the big wind."

"In his face all the way, if it travels that far. All the way from the fort."

He could picture Higgins, slumped low in the saddle, turning his head to catch his breath, and the horses with heads down, hating to face into the wind. Higgins had volunteered to see Brother Potter safe to the fort.

He went out of the tepee and caught up and saddled a horse and rode it across the frothy water and up on the benchlands. Give him a piece of canvas, he thought, and he and the horse could sail. It wasn't that he considered Higgins in danger. Higgins would make out all right. It was just that he would like to see him. It was just that he wanted to make sure. Horses could turn ornery, and badger holes could break legs.

The buffalo were returning from the south. He could make out four herds of them, sidewise to the wind, separate and mingling, then separating again as the leaders went their own ways. A world full of buffalo, but, even so, fewer than the bullets that would be fired. His horse flushed up a killdeer that fluttered briefly, sounding its two-toned cry, and ran off to the side on its thin, stilt legs. It was a wonder that all the birds, big and little, ground feeders and flycatchers, hadn't been swept from earth and sky and carried across the Missouri and way the hell beyond. He couldn't make out the figures of Higgins and the two horses though he willed his eyes to see over the lip of ground and sky. All he could see were buffalo and last year's grass thrashing.

He turned back, heading into the wind, and kicked his balky horse. The wind pushed at them like a hard, cold hand. It tore at his buckskins, swept his hair back, drove dust into his eyes and trapped the air in his lungs. Get along, horse. It ain't that far.

He got back to the tepees and unsaddled and went inside. To Teal Eye's asking look, he said, "Couldn't spot him, but he's on the way. Don't worry."

"I not worry about that. Not much."

"What then?"

"Not the wind. He needs a good woman. Not right, it is, for him to have not."

He smiled at her and put a hand on her head. She had a queer way of putting words, but it was something, how she had learned white man's talk. Nocansee spoke it, too, and Blackfoot to boot.

"Not everybody can be so lucky as me," he told Teal Eye, still smiling.

Now Nocansee spoke. "He will come when?"

"Sundown, I'm bettin'."

"I feel him gone."

"Yep. But just wait. Hey, the wind's easin' off."

The wind had slowed to a breeze, and smoke from the fire, over which Teal Eye had put a pot, rose straight through the smoke hole. That was the way in this breezy country, Summers thought. Some still days but mostly with the air moving soft and then, ever so often, a wind that tormented a man and made life hard for things trying to grow.

An hour or so later a voice called, "Anybody home?"

They went out, all of them, to greet Higgins. He looked like something the wind had had fun with before it passed on. The horses had stems of dead grass in their manes. "I'm a mite tattered," he said, "but Preacher Potter's all right, safe back at the fort."

"If you was any thicker with dust, I'd take you for sandstone," Summers told him. "Here. I'll see to the horses. You go down the river a ways and take off the top layer."

They ate and afterward sat outside on robes, the boys nearby, in the hour of no wind. More often than not, Summers thought, this was the way of it. Whether the day was windy or breezy or not, a time of stillness, of quiet, came soon after sundown. It was as if the day begged pardon for being so rough.

"I swear," Higgins said, "them young'ns have growed just while I been gone."

The boys sat beside Teal Eye, Lije quiet and safe between Nocansee's legs. With them that was usual.

Teal Eye had been waiting her time. Now she said to Higgins, "A good woman. That is it. A good woman you need."

"Truer words never came out of a mouth."

"We find you a woman."

"Now, lookee here. I ain't goin' to team up with just anybody. Not me. You got your mind on some Blackfoot girl you knowed from before?" Higgins sucked at his pipe.

Summers shook his head. "Nope. Not that."

"Why not? You done fine your own self."

"That was special." Summers nodded his head in agreement. "No Blackfoot for you, though."

"Why not?"

"Too close to home. Marry a Blackfoot woman and you marry into the tribe. All her relatives and friends will come visitin'. That's nice up to a point. Kind of fambly-like. But after a week of feedin' and entertainin' company, you find the doin's tiresome. You want 'em to be gone. But there'll come more kin and friends, eatin' your meat and all, makin' an Indian camp out of what we got. It's the way they think. What one's got, all's got. It's fair to say they'd treat you good if you visited them."

"Where's Teal Eye's kin, then?"

"They stay away," Teal Eye answered.

"Here's the how of it," Summers added. "All right I tell, Teal Eye?"

"Tell."

"When Teal Eye's white man killed his friend and took off, more'n a few bucks wanted her for their third or second or even their first wife. That didn't set good with her. She hit 'em and clawed 'em and fought 'em off and kept runnin' away. Finally they gave up and kind of outlawed her."

"Me, I have no people," Teal Eye said.

"Now whoa there. You got the boys and me and Hig. Ain't we people?"

She reached out to hold his hand. "My people," she said.

"So, barrin' the Blackfeet, where do we look?" Higgins asked.

"Away somewheres," Summers said. "I got me an idea. The Shoshones, now, they's lighter-hearted and merry and the women fair to the eye. I know 'em, some of 'em."

"Might not be for me."

"Might not, but I'm bettin' against it."

"How far? How many sleeps?" Higgins asked.

Summers shook his head. "It's a fair piece."

Teal Eye got to her feet. "We go then? Sunup come?" Summers felt a growing excitement in her.

"That might be pushin' things," he answered.

"You got a program? Somethin' else on your mind?" Higgins asked.

"I ain't sure."

"I wouldn't want to throw you off your stride," Higgins told him.

That was like Higgins, Summers thought. Always to put himself second. Like as not he knew what was in Summers' head. Find Boone Caudill — and then? Speak his piece and ride away? Make sense and right out of old wrongs? Why the damn itch?

Teal Eye said, "We go. Please, we go."

It struck him that she had been stuck here too long. She had taken care of the babies, done the cooking, kept the tepees clean and worked at what she shouldn't have but insisted on in spite of all orders. She might as well have been a damn slave. She needed to see folks. She needed change.

Put first things first, he told himself. Put Teal Eye first.

He rose to his feet. "Two sunups, and we break camp." Teal Eye clapped and ran to hug him. "Two sunups, and we go see can we find Higgins a wife."

21

Summers led away. Behind him came three pack horses, then Higgins with two, Teal Eye and the boys. He had mounted the boys on a gentle horse and, for lack of a saddle, had rigged a surcingle, with handholds, out of rope and a strip of hide. Lije rode in front of Nocansee, who held to the surcingle with one hand and the small boy with the other. They sure-God were safe enough. Both had been around horses and, as if to make up for his blindness, Nocansee had a great sense of balance. There were pack horses enough, more than enough, so that each was lightly loaded.

They splashed across the Teton near camp and set off down the wide valley. Light was flushing up from the eastern sky, and the meadowlarks, wakened, sang from the grasses. A good morning to set out. A good time to go before rain and the June rise of the rivers. Buffalo tramped along, going north, their hides rough with shedding hair. Calves trailed along, and wolves trailed behind, looking for a sick animal, or weakling, or for a chance at a cow giving birth.

Summers breathed deep, smelling buffalo and grass dew and horses and high-country air. These made a man. These kept him alive.

In country like this he had traveled with Jim Deakins and Caudill, and Deakins was full of funny questions about the why of things, about God's purposes and the end of it all. For him the end of it had come with a bullet.

He looked behind him to make sure of things and got a smile from Teal Eye. They would have to cross the Teton again and make for a saddle between a couple of buttes. The buttes stood ragged and bright, catching the first rays of the sun. He would steer clear of the mountains, much as he could, riding to the east of them, in time coming onto the Oregon Trail, which wouldn't be busy yet. Then on to White Hawk's band of Shoshones. He hoped White Hawk was still alive.

Boone Caudill, damn it and damn him. A good friend up to a point, but a friend only up to a point was no friend at all.

The far side of the Teton was rattlesnake country, and he called back to those behind him, "Horses might shy. Be ready! Snakes around here."

But it wasn't until they came to the saddle between the two buttes that they saw any snakes and then only a couple. Likely the weather was a mite cold for them yet.

They pressed on, veering east. Before sundown Summers decided to make camp close by a little gulch where spring water flowed. It was time. Teal Eye and the boys had begun to look peaked and were probably sore in their seats.

Dismounting, Summers said to Higgins, "Only risk here is snakes."

"Not wild-ass buffalo?"

"Nope."

Teal Eye was already off her horse and was helping the boys down. All of them would sleep under the sky tonight.

Summers and Higgins unloaded the pack horses and led them and the saddle stock down to drink. "Strange country to them," Summers said. "Better hobble 'em all."

"Yep."

Before they settled down, Summers walked circles around the camping place, making sure about snakes.

Teal Eye had a fire going and meat in a pot.

Higgins said, "Not an Injun so far, and nary a hide-hunter."

"Poor season for hides," Summers told him. "Old hair shed-din' off and the new not full-growed. Still, some will hunt."

"Where to tomorrow?"

"Across the Medicine, then across the Missouri."

"Every once in a while," Higgins said, gazing through the dusk and back to the mountains where the sun still lay on the peaks, "I think God was in a big way when he made this country."

It was something Jim Deakins might have said.

ㄱ ㄱ ㄱ

The Missouri lay behind them, the Missouri and the Yellow-stone and the Big Horn. Behind them were buttes and rolling plains and dry country thick with cactus. And here, on this sultry day, came the great migration of the buffalo. Here they were, hump after hump, horned heads and dull eyes. They came scattered and in close bunches, all moving north, and were slow to give way to the horses. They were like barnyard stock, Summers thought as his party rode south against the drift. It was as if their aim to move on had driven fear off.

Summers watched for dust. Even on spring turf a running herd would kick up a plume of it. Let a lightning bolt strike among them, or a few get startled over whatever, and the fun would start. There would be lowing and bawlings and the thunder of hoofs, and a man caught in the middle had best find a hole or a pole, or shoot enough animals to make a wall to lie behind.

He turned. Behind to his left rose a height of land crowned by a butte. "Keep your eye peeled, Hig," he said. "They get to runnin', and we'll all be pemmican."

Higgins grinned his crooked grin. "Without chokecherries to sweeten it."

Then, maybe half a mile ahead, Summers saw the first wave of dust. He saw animals bunching as they started to run, and those in front taking fright.

"Quick!" he called back, gesturing with an arm. "Turn back. Run with the herd. Slant off to the butte." He wrenched his horse around. "Turn, damn it!"

Teal Eye caught on, then Nocansee. Already Higgins had made his move. Summers dropped the pack rope. Let the pack horses take care of themselves. He moved up, said "Hang on," and with his rein ends lashed the horse that carried the boys.

The buffalo were all running now, ahead of them, at the sides and behind. "Slant off. Slant off, Teal Eye!" He smacked her horse.

He took the lead again. He stole a look back. Teal Eye was firm in the saddle, the boys still astride. Higgins had let loose of his pack horses. His voice rose hoarse, "Run, you bastards! Hi-yi. Hi-yi."

It was all thunder and dust and wild throat sounds now. Summers shot into a running bunch that blocked the way to the butte, and a cow fell and another fell over it, then another. He rode through the gap, his head turned to the rear. They had to make it. They were making it. Lije wore a big grin.

He reined around, poking a cow away with the muzzle of his gun. Here in the rear was the danger now, more than in front. The smell of sweating horses came to him, and a clot of horse lather flew back in his face. They were straining uphill, the horses winded but not slowing yet, and it seemed as if all of a sudden they were shut of the buffalo, well up on a butte where they could watch without risk.

The pack horses straggled up, their packs lopsided, none lost or turned under belly. The horses stood hipshot, cooling off. Teal Eye gave him a smile. Lije yelled, "Hi-yi," and Higgins grinned.

Higgins said, "To think them brutes is good to eat."

"I never seen 'em charge a butte yet."

◣ ◣ ◣

Over pipes that night Summers told Higgins, "We steer clear of the Big Horns."

"If that's them I see yonder, I vote aye."

"West of them is the place called Colter's Hell, where I never been. But south of there is Jackson's Hole, where I been more than once. Dave Jackson was a true mountain man."

Higgins blew out a stream of smoke. "Was? What happened to him?"

"Nobody knows. He was here and then he wasn't. He's not the only one."

No, not the only one, Summers thought. They came, the mountain men did, and some drowned and some starved and some froze. Some got rubbed out by Indians or died in fights among themselves. Some fell off passes or got kicked by a horse or killed by a bear, like old Hugh Glass, who was too tough to die, though, and made it back to the Missouri, wounds and all. It made a man wonder how come anybody was left.

Some died. No doubt about that. Mostly they died unbeknownst, with no graves to mark them, no signposts saying who, what or why. But would they have done different, knowing ahead? Likely not.

They rode on the next day. It was a fair day, not bothersome hot, and birds sang and plants bloomed, and after a while they would find Higgins a wife.

◣ ◣ ◣

The sun was touching the western mountains when Summers saw smoke. It could be the smoke of Crows or Blackfeet or Sioux or who knew what. He reined in his horse. Higgins rode up beside him. "I ain't of a mind to circle around," Summers said. "We was bound to meet Indians when we took off. But we ain't a war party and got nothin' much to fear unless losin' a horse."

Teal Eye had come up to look. "A man we could lose," she said. "Sioux mean people." She took Summers' arm. "Please, we go round."

"Now, little duck," he answered, "you know me. I'm careful." With his arm he squeezed her hand against his ribs. "How else would I live so long?"

She shook her head, asking please without saying it, and for a moment, moved by her concern, he thought of agreeing. But there couldn't be any real danger, so he answered, "We'll be all right."

It was a camp, he saw as they drew nearer, of maybe thirty tepees. From the layout he guessed it was Blackfoot. The Indian dogs began to bark.

A man walked toward them, unarmed. Summers got off his horse and handed his Hawken to Higgins. He stepped toward the man, making the peace sign. The man was Blackfoot all right. His different beaded moccasins told that. He wore old buckskins. His hair was plaited without so much as a feather in it, nor was there paint on his face. He might be fifty or so years old.

Summers said, "How," as the man made the peace sign.

"How," the man answered. He put a pointing finger to his chest, "Heavy Runner, me."

"Dick Summers, me."

The man's dark, squinched-up eyes examined him. "You are Bear Maker. No?" Summers nodded. "You have the Blackfoot wife?"

"Teal Eye, her name."

They had been talking partly with hands, partly with voices. Summers went on, "You are chief. I know from the big fort."

"Come. My lodge. We will smoke."

Summers waved a come-on to his mates and waited for them. When Teal Eye came up, she said, "It is Blackfoot camp. Not my friends."

"It's Chief Heavy Runner. He's got nothin' against you."

Men, women and children, having word from the chief, began moving toward them from the camp. Dogs trotted along with them. Indians always had dogs.

After the business of getting acquainted and getting settled was over, Summers and Higgins and a couple of head men smoked in Heavy Runner's lodge that night. Summers said, asking, "It is not yet the time of the hunt. It is not the chief's hunting ground."

Heavy Runner considered before he spoke in words and signs. "It is the hunting ground of nobody, so of everybody." He drew on the pipe. "We were smoking with the Arapahoes, our friends, but the young men got to fighting — "

"It is the way of young men."

The head men were silent, waiting on the chief's words. Heavy Runner passed the pipe. "You are my friends. My camp is your camp and my lodge your lodge."

"And my tobacco your tobacco." Summers took two plugs from his pocket and passed them over. From the smell of the pipe, he reckoned their tobacco had been kinnikinnick or red-willow bark, for lack of the real thing.

"Tell me," Heavy Runner said after he had put the plug on a board and got out his knife, "the Great Father try to say this land is your land, that land those men's, and another to another. I am friend of the paleface, but I do not understand."

"I live the red man's life, and I do not know."

"So the land is ours, but the white man still comes. He builds his own lodges where we are owners. He kills our buffalo. Sometimes he kills us. He moves on our land, scratching for the yellow metal. It is part of the land. Yes? It belongs to us. I cannot understand."

The chief had the pipe going and took note with it of the four directions before passing it on.

Summers thought God himself couldn't answer the questions, much less the Great Father. "The white men are many," he said, "and I do not know what the moons will bring."

Lying with Teal Eye that night, Summers thought he was anyhow partway a liar. He knew what the moons would bring, if not the all of it. But if there was no all-out answer, there was a downright fact. People. All of them wanting land or riches or maybe just a handhold on life. Come down to it, he thought and grinned a sour grin inside himself, he was a mite greedy himself, wanting the land kept open and free just for his sake.

22

THE SWEETWATER and the Oregon Trail, winding plain to the eye but untraveled yet, the season being early. Independence Rock and the Devil's Gate, just as Summers remembered them, and then on to South Pass, with the Wind River mountains rising high to the right.

It would be good to poke along the Popo Agie or the Wind, thinking to be setting traps again and each one sprung soon, each lift heavy with beaver. The water was cold enough to paralyze a man's privates, but who cared? Who cared when the spring season was good and rendezvous just around the corner, where a man could drink around campfires and trade lies and find squaws? Who thought of age then? Who gave a damn? Who saw the end of a life?

But this thinking was wrong, this remembering, this hankering. Would he trade the life he was leading for the life he had led? Would he give up Teal Eye and the boys and Higgins in order to turn back the years? Not by a damn sight. Teal Eye had changed him, he thought, Teal Eye and family had changed him. If his mind was rich and sad with remembering, it was rich and good with what he had. Sure, things would change. But change, for better or worse, was the damned order of life.

He hitched in the saddle to make sure the string was all right.

Yep. People were coming. He couldn't fight that. Every man had the same rights that he did. Let every man make his mistakes, as he had done when he was young. Looking at the wooded hills, at the mountain meadows thick with grass, both empty now of all but wildlife, he figured there weren't enough whites in the country to ruin it all. Something would remain. A great deal of what he saw in the shimmering distances would remain, hardly touched and unspoiled. Teal Eye had softened him all right. Whatever fret he felt he would keep to himself, knowing how useless it was. The buffalo would go. That seemed likely, but the hills would still be in place and the streams flowing.

South Pass, an easy climb and drop with Pacific Springs at the end of it. Sublette's Cutoff to the Seeds-kee-dee or Prairie Hen River, which people were calling the Green. A long haul and dry, that cutoff, but easier with saddle and pack horses than with oxen and wagons. Discarded stuff along the way — an anvil, a big cherry press, bins and boxes, an earthenware crock — the plunder that made loads too heavy for sore-footed pullers.

One thing stuck in his gizzard, too heavy to pass through his system. Jim Deakins dead and Boone Caudill the killer. He had pieced the story together, from Birdwhistle there on the Columbia's banks, from Higgins who told him the talk at Fort Benton, from Teal Eye when she would speak of it. Caudill, the sudden and unthinking man, had shot Deakins out of suspicion with no hold on fact. He had killed his friend and deserted Teal Eye and the boy and not set foot in Blackfoot country again. He had to be told the truth somehow and somewhere. He had to live with his mistake. That was fair. All men should live with the wrongs they had done.

It pricked him a little, thinking of Teal Eye sleeping with Caudill. But Teal Eye was Teal Eye. Nothing could spoil her. She had shut Caudill out of her mind, or tried to. When Summers pushed her about him, she talked little and then in a half-strangled voice.

Now down to the Bear, down the steep slope of it where Oregon wagons had had to be wheel-locked and lowered with ropes.

"Shoshone country," Summers said to Higgins. "You'll be took by surprise. They're lighter complected than you would expect, nigh light as Mandans, them as was all killed off by the smallpox. Watch out you don't flush up a bride."

"Should I take a pot shot or shoot her on the wing?"

"Just smile a pretty smile."

"I'm thinkin' brides is as skeerce as buffalo in this country."

"We'll trail up Smith's Fork. Time was, maybe still is, that White Hawk liked to camp around there."

They came to an old camp where fires had burned, and the grass grew different where tepees had stood.

A couple of miles farther on Summers spotted a horse herd on a hillside and two men standing watch. The trail led down into a basin. In the center of it tepees rose, rusty white in the sun. "I'm thinkin' we reached the end of the trip," Summers said.

He led down toward the tepees, making the peace sign as he went, and dogs barked and faces turned, and a man came out of the biggest tepee and faced them, squinting.

He was White Hawk, Summers made out, White Hawk with years on him and many moons in his face. Summers slid from his horse. "White Hawk, my brother," he said. "I bring tobacco and beads."

A slow look of knowing came into White Hawk's eyes, and time seemed to shed from him. "My brother," he cried out. "Dick Summers, my white brother." He stepped forward to shake hands and, as if the shake wasn't enough, took Summers by the arm.

The Indians gathered around, men dressed in patches of leather and cloth, women in their shapeless sacks save for a couple in calico and children bare-assed as the day they were born. They set up a clamor, merry as birds in a fresh-turned field.

White Hawk said, using signs but words, too, "All belong you. The camp. My lodge. Meat in the pot." He kicked lightly at a dog that was sniffing Summers.

"I have my wife, my sons and my good friend. Higgins his name."

"We are happy. Come."

"Packs first, and the horses."

White Hawk turned to a couple of young men and spoke in Shoshone. To Summers he said, "They take care. No steal from you. I have spoken."

Seated by White Hawk's fire outside his lodge, they ate deer meat seasoned with sage and other flavorings Summers couldn't name. The chief's two wives bustled around, making sure the men were well fed, watching the fire to keep the pot hot. With them was a young girl, pretty and uncommonly fair, who was too young to be wife to old White Hawk. But maybe not.

The sun winked out behind the hills, and a mild chill came on. A coyote, singing, set the camp dogs to barking.

"We are too many for your lodge, brother," Summers said. "We have lodges. All right to set them up next to yours?"

"Where you want. Me, I say the camp is yours." He rose to his feet, his legs stiff and awkward with age. "Come. We smoke."

Inside the lodge, where a small fire was taking hold, White Hawk loaded the pipe, lit it with a twig from the fire, pointed it in the four directions and passed it to Summers, who puffed and handed the pipe to Higgins.

"You hunt the buffalo still? Across the mountains?" Summers asked.

White Hawk bent his head. His voice was low. "For these moons I think no. It is bad. Bad medicine last hunt."

Summers kept silent, sure the chief would go on.

"My son." He rubbed the fingers of one hand in the palm of the other. "He is with me no more."

"He fight?"

"His horse stumble and fall in the hunt. Buffalo pound him."

"My heart is sad for you," Summers said, noting how much English the chief had picked up.

"His woman I take into my lodge. His little squaw, too."

"His daughter?"

"My — what you say?"

"Granddaughter."

The chief made the sign for yes, bowing his body as well as his head.

"By the fire I see her?"

Again the chief signed a yes.

"You have learned much white man's talk."

"By the Bear. By the trail. They come. Many come, and I talk. Has the white man no hunting ground from where he come? How many is he?"

"Like the blades of grass. Like the leaves on the trees. They come to shoot. No buffalo on their range. They come to plow. The new soil in Oregon, it is better."

The chief sighed a sort of spent sigh, then straightened and asked, "Why you come?"

"To see my brother."

"That is good. That is all?"

Summers turned a thumb toward Higgins. "Here is a good man. They call him Friend of the Great Bear. He has no woman."

"Say to him he will have one. I make sure."

"Not that way, my brother. A wife he wants. One to keep. He is not rough man, but kind."

For a long moment Chief White Hawk studied Higgins, who shifted under his stare. "He is too old. Old. No teeth."

"Not too old." Summers figured, knowing Higgins, that it was fair to lie. "He take tomahawk in the mouth. A Sioux it was. He killed the Sioux, Higgins did."

"And his mouth broken?"

"Yes. Broken mouth and all."

"What woman he want?" the chief asked, looking with more favor at Higgins.

"He does not say yet. He is just come. But I see many young women in camp."

The chief sat as if heavy with thought. "Our women good, no?"

"It is true. Good-looking women. Good wives, I say."

"I will think."

Now Summers dared to say, "That one I saw and think how pretty, there by your fire."

"Little Wing. Granddaughter."

"If she has no man, I say to you, Higgins is a good man, he is. He not be cruel like some. He be kind."

The chief smoked and looked at the wall of the lodge as if into distance. What went on in his head didn't show in his face. At last he said, "We are poor."

"You know the yellow metal?"

"Paleface, he love it. I know."

Summers held out the last three pieces of gold he had earned as a guide. "For a wife?"

"It is not horses."

"It buy horses. It buy eight, ten, twelve. That is enough, yes, my brother?"

For a long time White Hawk gazed into the bed of coals that had been a fire. He tossed a stick on them. "It is true. My Little

Wing has no man. Many want her, but they have not the horses. I will ask her, but if she say no?"

"I will ask my friend, too. I do not know how he feels."

White Hawk let a little smile come on his face. "No man say no to her."

After they had left the lodge, Higgins asked, "Now what in the hell was that all about? I just catched a word now and then."

"I was dickerin' for a wife for you."

"Just any old wife, huh? Just anything?"

"You seen her."

"Who? Where?"

"That pretty filly by the campfire, that one with the two older women."

"Jesus Christ! She wouldn't go for the likes of me."

"Women don't have much say in this business. The father or grandfather or brother decides, dependin' on how many horses he gets."

Higgins stopped Summers in his tracks. "I won't have it, by God! She has to be willin', more'n willin', or it's no go with me. Got that?"

"Simmer down. We got Teal Eye to make sure. You just play your fiddle and sing."

23

THE CAMP came alive early. Squaws were bringing in wood, building fires, filling pots and kettles while children played. Their voices sounded in steady, good-natured chatter. Mostly the men sat at the flaps of the tepees, doing nothing but wait.

"The bucks sure got it easy," Higgins said to Summers. "Like as if it would hurt them to do some of the chores."

Higgins had gathered wood for Teal Eye while the men watched, their faces showing so little that they showed much. A man doing squaw's work! Summers had seen to the horses and fetched water. Now Teal Eye was tending a pot. The boys were in back of her, Lije holding to Nocansee's hand.

It had been Teal Eye's doing that they had their own fire and fixed their own food. "We come to visit, yes," she had said. "But not to sit and eat their meat."

Higgins was watching the chief's fire and the girl who busied herself there. He said, "It won't work."

"What?" Summers asked, knowing the answer.

"Me'n her, that's what. Damned if I push."

"Who's askin' you to? We got Teal Eye."

"I tell her about you," Teal Eye said to Higgins. "I find out."

"Why the all-fired hurry? Could be I won't like her."

"Could be," Teal Eye answered, making a grave face.

The night chill was easing off as the day lightened. Soon the sun would be up. On the hillside the horses were frisking, running and kicking up to get the kinks out or to welcome the light.

"I'm puttin' you on for tonight," Summers said.

"Who said you could?"

"For fiddle music and singin'."

"Jesus Christ! I got no say, huh?"

"Nope."

Higgins shook his head, saying, "I just might get balky."

"Cheer up. After we've et, we go huntin'."

"They do their own huntin'."

"Yep. But not a rifle in camp. Just a few old smoothbores that ain't accurate for more'n three or four jumps. Them and bows and arrers."

"We all the same as camp hunters?"

"It don't hurt to bring in meat. I'm bettin' the hunters will stick in camp, waitin' to see how we come out."

They ate and went to bring in their horses — two for saddles and three for packs. Hobbled, the horses weren't hard to catch.

Back in camp, they threw on the saddles. Summers said to Teal Eye, "Back before you know it, back with much meat."

She gave him the smile she smiled for him alone and came forward and touched his arm. "I wait for you. All the time."

They mounted, rifles held crosswise in front of them. Passing White Hawk in front of his lodge, Summers said, "We kill meat. What your mouth say?"

"It is long time since sheep. Long time since bighorn. Maybe you find one. My hunters have hard time. Far for the arrow."

Little Wing came from the lodge. She threw a look at Higgins, who sat stiff as a stick, holding his rifle.

They rode out of the valley into the hills, Summers saying, "Sheep he wants. Sheep in this country. I don't know. Plenty elk and deer, though."

They followed a game trail, winding uphill. The horses, not pushed, snatched for wild berries and the crowns of bull thistles. The sun, barely up, was at their backs, the breeze in their faces. Overhead the sky was deep, but a man couldn't see its far rims, not with hills and trees closing them off.

"Hell of a place to hunt," Higgins said. "Brush and stuff all around, and any game, spottin' us, be lost to sight before we could aim."

"Game trails lead to somethin', to a lick or an open meadow. That's where they're like to be."

"Or lyin' up somewheres, their bellies full."

"You're as cheerful as a hell's fire preacher. Buck up. Fine day today."

No use, Summers thought. Higgins' lips were set in a tight, crooked line.

Through the trees Summers caught a glimpse of a clearing. "Let's tie up. Goin' afoot is the ticket now, I'm thinkin'."

It was as he had figured, a small park in the trees with a pool of water close to its middle. They approached, stooping, and lay down at the edge.

The meadow was green, with hardly a bush in it, only grass and more grass, spotted here and there with a flower of some kind. Nothing moved in it except for a crowned jay, dark blue, that flew over it and perched in a pine. Nothing moved but little butterflies, mosquitoes and a swarm of gnats. There was the voice of silence, the far thrum that sounded deep in the ear.

"It ain't a good time of day," Higgins said.

"Who knows, savin' the critters themselves?"

They waited while the sun rose higher. It didn't have much heat in it yet. Summers chewed on a grass stem. Half of hunting was waiting. Higgins had put his head on his arms. He might be sleeping.

The mosquitoes buzzed thick. They didn't bother Summers much. His skin was too old and leathery, he figured. He waited, unmoving, his Hawken lying in front of him.

His eyes hunted for movement. Sure to God there was game around here. Elk and deer at the least. He had seen their tracks on the trail. Mountain sheep maybe. Across the divide they were plenty enough, and mountain men, froze for good meat when buffalo were scarce, had found sheep tasty and good in the belly.

On a ridge beyond the meadow he caught a flicker of action. He squinted. Three, no, four gray-white blobs, moving slow, coming down to feed and to drink. He nudged Higgins and pointed with a finger. Higgins raised his head and stared and finally nodded. He didn't quite have the hunter's eye.

The sheep stepped dainty down the ridge, on guard but not spooky. Two looked like good meat. They came within range of the Hawken but not of the Kentucky. He said, low-voiced to Higgins, "Hold up. Aim at the small one to the right. Fire when I say go."

Careful in his movements, he planted the ramrod, held it with his left hand and laid the gun across his arm for a rest. Higgins had the lighter rifle at his shoulder.

"Go!"

The animal he had aimed at fell without a quiver. Higgins' target jumped once and scrambled and lay still. The two older sheep ran off.

They reloaded their rifles. "Good fare for White Hawk," Summers said.

"Won't feed the camp."

"Could be we ain't done."

They walked back and got the horses and rode to the dead sheep. They skinned and gutted them, saving the fleeces, and, with the carcasses wrapped in canvas and hitched to a pack horse, they sat down and smoked.

The sun had begun its slide to the west. One white cloud, round as a bullboat, sailed in the east. The breeze died out.

It was then that a single elk walked out of the woods. Summers whispered, "If I don't knock it dead, you fire." Aiming without a rest, it flicked into his mind that he should let Higgins shoot. But the Kentucky was small for an elk.

The elk grunted to the smack of the bullet, walked hunched a few feet and lay down.

"Plenty meat now," Summers said.

It was going on to dusk when they got back to camp, their pack horses loaded. And it was as if the whole damn camp came out to meet them, children forgetting their play, women forgetting their fires and men forgetting to loaf.

They rode to White Hawk's lodge. He had come out and stood in front of it, pleasure showing in his old face.

"He bring you sheep," Summers said, pointing to Higgins. "Two sheep, one elk we have, for you and your people."

White Hawk moved his right hand and held his extended fingers to his left breast, then fluttered the hand in a plane to his right. It was the sign for good. Maybe it also meant thanks.

The women got busy unloading the meat, their voices raised in pleased chatter. One of them was Little Wing. Higgins said, "For Christ sake," to Summers and moved as if to take the girl's place. Summers grabbed him by the arm. "That won't win you no ribbons. Don't butt in. Let it go."

Teal Eye came up with the boys in tow. "Big hunter," she said, putting her hand on his sleeve. "I am proud."

"You keep out of the way, little duck. I'll unload."

At his side Higgins said, "That won't win you no ribbons."

Summers glanced at him, then at Teal Eye, and said, "I already won mine."

Teal Eye pulled at his sleeve. "The other women do it. Shame to me."

Summers smiled. "Grab that rope then. Last thing I want is to shame you."

The women began cutting and hacking at the carcasses. There was no quarreling, no grabbing, or not much, for the best cuts. They just divvied the meat even, a share for each fire. Teal Eye took a chunk and walked toward their lodge. She hadn't fussed or grabbed, but still it was sheep meat she carried, knowing that he liked it for a change.

◣ ◣ ◣

That night they sat in a rough circle in front of the lodges — men, women and young'ns. The lean dogs limped around, sniffing for scraps. There was a time of waiting. Indians were good at waiting.

Summers took Higgins by the arm. In the other hand Higgins carried his fiddle. "Mosey out to the center, sit down and make music," Summers said.

"Christ, Dick, I ain't no prize at a box social. You rigged this deal, but damn if I like it. I'd druther take off or crawl in a hole."

Under Summers' hand Higgins' arm trembled. "Now, now, Hig. You can do 'er. You know you can do 'er. I know it. Teal Eye knows it. You wouldn't let her down, or Little Wing, either. She's there in front of the chief's lodge. Go it, boy."

"Oh, shit."

Higgins walked out slow but not bent, like a brave man knowing he was about to get shot. He took his time sitting down. He took his time tuning the fiddle. His first tunes were quick and merry, and the hands and feet of the Indians moved to the rhythms. "Sing, damn you," Summers said without speaking. "Fiddle alone ain't enough. Sing."

As Higgins paused, the Indians' voices rose, thanking him, wanting more. Higgins sat still, the bow upheld in his right hand, as if waiting for word from inside himself. Summers reckoned his flutter had died.

Higgins lowered the bow, took a couple of slow licks and sang, low-voiced at first. He sang old songs, dim and far back in Summers' memories, songs of lost love and death, sorrowful as years that had passed. Voice and fiddle, gaining strength, seemed to move around the tepees, seemed to move to the still trees and carry on into distance.

The Indians sat without moving. Smoke wavered up from dying campfires. The tepees rose shadowed under a slanting half-moon.

Summers knew he was breathing short and slow, as if even the sound of breathing was out of place. Little Wing sat like a statue. Even the two boys at his feet didn't fidget. A dog let out a mournful howl and was cuffed into silence.

Voice and fiddle. They sang all the lonesomeness of time, the sad lonesomeness of the years, the sad, sweet lonesomeness. Teal Eye's hand reached out and took his.

Higgins got up to the cry of voices and walked to his tepee, not paying heed. The Indians, silent now, watched, unmoving, as if it was right to leave the singer alone.

Summers put his arm around Teal Eye and pressed her against him. "Some doin's," he said and knew how poor the words were.

24

S HE SAY YES," Teal Eye said.

That didn't mean that Little Wing was all for marrying him, Higgins thought. Maybe she was just paying mind to the chief who, thinking of horses, had given his orders. Maybe she was just being biddable. That was one hell of a way to pick out a mate.

It was dark and late and a trifle chill, and he sat around the fire with Summers and Teal Eye. The boys had gone to bed.

"Could be she's just bowin' to White Hawk," Higgins said. "Like as if she had to."

"No, she like you. It is not the chief, not the horses."

So she liked him, huh? Liked him with age coming on him. Liked him with his haggle of mouth. It didn't stand to reason.

He said, "Dick buys me a bride out of his own pocket."

"Shut up," Summers told him, smiling.

If he had teeth like Summers, it might be different. If he looked like Summers, face and body, it might be.

"I ain't goin' to, Dick," he said. "This is plenty important. Why is she willin' to marry me? On account of the chief? On account of I'm white?"

Teal Eye put in, "Because you are you."

"Just bein' white don't mean anything. Underneath any color, there's just blood and meat."

"And brains and hearts," Summers said.

"I seen enough black-hearted white men."

"We're off the track, seems to me."

"I reckon I know what I know."

"It's only you knows things," Summers said. He grinned as if to take the raw off his words. "But if it ain't a go with you, then it's no go."

"I didn't say that."

"It's about how I got it."

"Oh, hell, Dick. She's pretty and she seems all right, but I don't know."

"Foolish man, you," Teal Eye said. "She make good wife."

They sat silent then, as if more words were no use. They stared into the fire. A thing about fire, Higgins thought. In the flicker of it, in the small leaps of flame, men might think they'd find answers. In it they dreamed dreams, dreams of happiness, dreams of peace, the ends of hankerings. Was it the same way with Indians? Not now for sure since the other fires were dead and their people asleep. But still, what did fire mean to them, other than warmth and heat to cook by? Were their dreams of warpath and scalps? Or did they, like him, just want their frets gone?

He looked up at the sky, seeing nothing but black overcast. The Shoshone tepees blended into the dark. A horse whickered from the hillside, and a coyote sang to the night, bark and quaver and trill.

He felt a small burrowing at his side and flinched and

reached out, and his hand closed on a small hand, and he looked quick, and there was Little Wing, her eyes catching the glow of the fire. He kept hold of the hand.

The fire, and a hand in his, and Summers and Teal Eye watching, silent, knowing as he did that she had come on her own, slipping out to them while the camp slept.

The fire, and a hand in his, and he said, his voice rough in his ears, "When can we do it, Dick?"

"Camp's awake before sunup. How about sunup?"

"Tomorrow?"

"Tomorrow. I'll talk to the chief."

"Tell her — no, ask her if it's all right."

Summers spoke to her in Shoshone, and she answered, and then the hand drew away from his, and she was lost in the dark.

"They got a ceremony, Dick. A rigmarole?"

"Search me. Maybe they get out their rattles. Maybe march with their coup sticks. Maybe so a dance or more."

"Rattles rattlin'. Drums thumpin'. Hi-yi and hi-yi. You got to save me from that, Dick."

"No help for it, fur as I can see."

"I got an idee."

"So?"

"You marry us. You be the preacher."

Summers' mouth opened, and then he laughed, keeping the laugh low so as not to be heard in the tepees. "That's the damndest thing these ears ever heard. Me playin' preacher!"

"You got your marriage license?"

"Sure thing."

"Show it. Make as if you were reading from it. The camp won't know any different. And maybe, between us, we can piece out the Lord's Prayer."

"I'm thinkin' you're out of your mind."

"No, Dick. What you might say would be as bindin' on me as a double-tied rope, tight as any preacher could make it."

"Who says the camp would go along?"

"White Hawk listens to you. I'm bettin' the Indians would

be — what is it? — impressed. They would be plumb pleased. Do it, Dick, please."

Teal Eye put in, "I think right. My man will do it. Yes?"

Summers put a hand on her head and gave it a small shake. "Even you vote against me. I'm elected, huh? I never thought to ride so close to God."

"You mean you will?"

"Looks like I got to, no matter what. Means I have to talk to the chief and set it up, if I can, before sunshine."

In his bed that night Higgins stayed awake for a while, going over his lingering doubts. He couldn't even talk the girl's talk, barring a few words. She couldn't talk his. How could one know what the other was thinking, what the other one wanted? Coupling was one thing, but where was the real glue? It lay deeper than talk, he thought. It lay in the feelings. It lay in wishing only good for the other. A man could call it love if he wanted to.

◣ ◣ ◣

Higgins got up before light. He went to the stream and cleaned himself and put on fresh clothes, and, back in his lodge, shaved by feel in the dark, using his old straight edge, cold water and the scrap of soap he had saved from his bath.

Teal Eye called to him and came in when he said to, leaving open the flap of the tepee. There was just enough light to see close-up things by. She had him sit down, and she kneeled behind him and braided his moist hair, tying red ribbons at the ends.

She was almost done when Summers came in. He looked almost white in his best buckskins. "I got it fixed," he said. "Chief's agreeable, but he wants to stand by me, which is all right. He wised up the camp. The Lord's Prayer is pretty well set in my head."

"What else you aimin' to say?"

"What comes to mind. Now rest easy. It's me actin' beyond my own self. It ain't easy, puttin' myself in the pulpit."

"You seen Little Wing?"

"She'll be ready."

When Higgins looked out of the tepee, he saw that dawn had sneaked up on the dark. The bowl of the sky had turned silver except for a kindle of fire in the east. He sat cross-legged and waited. A man couldn't hurry up time. The women were getting up but not building fires.

Summers passed by him, saying he would come back when the time came. Higgins kept waiting, feeling empty of stomach and raw in his nerves. The sun, not yet up, had laid a red banner before it. People had begun ranking themselves, men first, then women, then children.

Teal Eye appeared, bringing Little Wing, who smiled a kind of scared smile. Her hand took his. They walked out. The Indians stood, their eyes alive, their bodies still.

Teal Eye led them to where Summers stood. White Hawk was beside him, wearing his eagle-feather headdress. Teal Eye faded back.

"Step ahead, please," Summers said. "Turn a little. Let light be on your faces." He looked around at the crowd and spoke for a while in Shoshone. When he couldn't find a word, he made the sign for it.

The sun, half up now, caught the silver in Summers' hair. The white of the marriage license Summers held in his hand seemed to make White Hawk's dark skin even darker. Higgins felt the girl's hand tremble in his.

Summers switched into English. "I have explained the white man's way. One wife and her forever."

Uh-huh, Higgins thought. That's what the book says. So what? He would go by the book.

"I have said that was your way, Mr. Higgins, that you were a good man and would make a good husband. Now let's get on with it."

He looked at the license, then raised both hands. "Let the sun see, and the moon and stars at night. Let the winds, big and little, take notice."

By God, Higgins thought, there were more sides to Dick
Summers than to broken ice. And he was serious, not sly or
playful as Higgins had feared. He was sober enough himself,
but Summers' words made him more so. He pressed the girl's
hand.

"With the blessing of the great spirit, this man and this
woman are about to be wed."

He explained in Shoshone.

"Let your blessings be on them."

Again the Shoshone.

Using both languages together with gestures, Summers went
on, "If anybody's got any reason against this marriage, speak
up now or shut up forever."

He looked over the crowd, then turned to Higgins and said
as if reading from the marriage license, "Do you, Hezekiah Higgins, take this woman to be your wife, your wife all the time,
your only wife?"

Higgins turned to Little Wing and saw her mouth and lips
moving soundlessly as he spoke. "I do that."

"And you, Little Wing, do you take this man to be your husband, through sickness and health and whatever comes?"

She answered, plain as day, "I do that."

"Then I say — and let everyone hear me — I say you are
man and wife." He bent his head and said the Lord's Prayer
without a mistake.

"Now, Chief White Hawk?"

White Hawk held out his hands and said something Higgins
couldn't understand.

Summers' voice followed. "Hug her, Hig. Kiss her, you fool."

Higgins had to put up with a day of feasting, a day of talk,
a day of smoking. Morning and afternoon wore on, and dusk
came and then dark. He wasn't sure whether he led Little Wing
to his lodge or she led him. Teal Eye or Summers or both had
repitched the tepee, far enough away from others for privacy.
They entered and closed the flap.

25

"WE MOVE," White Hawk had said. "Camp stink."

Higgins couldn't say no to that. They had passed last summer in the same spot and then winter, and now another summer was coming along. Too long, he thought, for people who squatted and did their business on the outskirts of camp. In the summer they kept themselves clean by dowsing in the stream. In the winter they made do with cold water or snow. That didn't remove the smell of their leavings, not with warm weather at hand.

"It is time," Summers had answered. He wouldn't say it was past time, though it was. He wouldn't mention that the women had to go farther and farther for firewood, knowing the chief knew it, too. Summers' thumb moved to his words. "Downstream or up?"

They were speaking mostly in Shoshone, which Higgins had got some of the hang of.

"Down. Old camp dry and sweet now."

"To the Bear?"

"No. White-man road too close."

He meant the shortcut and the Oregon Trail, Higgins knew. Pretty soon the prairie schooners would begin rolling. For all he knew, they were rolling already.

Let them roll. Let farmers and clerks and businessmen and preachers and sharpers hit the trail. Just leave the Shoshones alone. It was a good life he was leading with them, good with Little Wing as his wife and Summers and his family as close friends. Who the hell wanted more, unless it might be to see the high plains again and eat buffalo meat? They had fallen into a pattern, he and Summers. For the most part they supplied meat for the camp, going out almost day by day and bringing back elk, deer or sheep and once in a while, for variety, a black bear. Sometimes they took an Indian or two with them and let them try their luck with the Hawken or the Kentucky and so made friends in the camp.

It seemed that some of Summers' old twitch had left him. For months he had appeared easy in mind, pleased enough just to hunt or loaf around camp or spend time with his boys. Once, last summer, he had ridden down to the Bear, just to see, he said, how many were the wagon trains, how many took the shortcut, how many went by way of Fort Bridger. That's what he had said, but Teal Eye had doubt in her eyes.

So they had struck their lodges and moved downstream, the women doing the work of taking down tepees, fixing the lodge poles for travois, packing the horses that the men brought in. Little Wing had come to the point where she let him help some. The horse herd, moved by five or six riders, would bring up the rear.

They made quite a procession, Higgins thought, riding just ahead of the herd — loose horses, saddle horses, pack animals, men, women, children, dogs, all dusting the way to new grounds.

Once they were settled, Higgins said to Summers, "Thought I'd ride down to where the cutoff meets the Bear."

"Take a couple of days."

"I reckon Little Wing will bear up. She's tannin' hides. Me, I'd like to see what's doin' with the palefaces. Care to come along?"

Summers shook his head. "'Nother time, maybe. Right now me and the boys have some plans."

Higgins rode off alone at the first flush of light. The night's chill faded as the day woke up. The season was coming full — full of leaf and bloom, squirrels busy, birds, too, singing hello to a new day. An eagle let out a scream. He could just see it, a dot in the far sky. He rode through a growth of quaking asps, in full leaf now, the leaves trembling to the breath of no wind. It was shady beneath them, cool and shady, and nothing could ever kill them but thirst. He could tie up here and smoke a pipe and say to hell with the world's doings while his eye rested on green leaves and white bark. But he hankered to know. It would be a change just to talk to white strangers, to hear about their trip, to get outside news.

It was the edge of dark when he cut away from Smith's Fork to strike the Bear River north of the shortcut, and he watered his horse, picketed it in good grass, ate jerky from his saddle bag and lay down for the night. Tomorrow he might kill some meat.

Birds, singing their heads off, wakened him at dawn. His horse was all right. He had a drink of water for breakfast and was on his way. Summers had reminded him he would have to ford the Bear twice to cut through the loop it made to the north. All right. He could do it, or his horse could.

To the south of him now he could see the shimmer of Bear Lake. A couple of deer flushed up, and he swung his rifle up and around before thinking the day was too young and hot yet. There were plenty of deer.

He shot a small, fat one just before the second crossing of the Bear, where he would meet the real Oregon Trail and turn south for the point where the cutoff came in. He took out the scent glands and gutted the deer, saving the liver. He tied the carcass behind his saddle. There would be waste unless he found someone to help eat it.

The way was longer than he remembered, and it was along toward dusk before he arrived.

Four horses stood where the cutoff and the Bear met, two grounded riders beside them. The men had a fire going on a patch of bare shore. Their unloaded packs lay on the ground, unopened. They were young men who looked older because of their beards. They looked fagged, too. The horses, having drunk, still nosed at the water. He rode up and said, "Howdy, strangers."

The men nodded, saying nothing, but seemed not unfriendly.

"Bound for Oregon? Right?"

They looked at each other, and one of them asked, "What makes you think so?"

"I took the trail myself onct."

"Cutoff included?"

"Yup. With wagons. It was teetotal hell."

"Hard enough with horses. Eh, Dan?"

Dan said, "Sure is," and rubbed his butt.

"Mind if I get off my horse a while?"

"Suit yourself," the other man said.

Higgins dismounted, slanted his Kentucky against a stone and reached for his pipe.

"I was some disappointed in Oregon," he said.

"Too bad, but not our worry."

"No?"

Dan turned to fiddle with one of the packs, saying, "Ask Walt."

Walt was the bigger of the two men. They were city boys, Higgins figured, but not city-bred. Probably farm boys to begin with.

"We're bound for California," Walt said.

"Californy, huh?"

"And the gold that's there."

"Gold!"

Dan turned from the pack. "Where you been, old-timer?"

"Not where I heerd anything like that. Gold?"

"In every stream and every gulch. That's the word. Came to us almost firsthand. Sit down. Light your pipe. We're too damn tired to eat yet."

"Figured you could help me eat that deer there."

"Thanks. Fresh meat, Walt."

"Makes me hungry to think of it."

They were all seated now. Higgins passed a blazing stick he had lighted his pipe with.

"We got a long jump on most folks," Dan said between puffs. "Heard the news early and gave up our jobs, bought horses and set out. But it's like the whole nation was on the move or soon will be, all headed for California."

"Not all, Dan. There's the Mormons."

"If you want to call them folks."

"Anyhow, some's already on the trail, but not after gold. They're headed for their settlement on what's called Great Salt Lake, goin' by Fort Bridger."

"Mormons," Higgins said. "There was trouble in Missouri afore I left."

Both men nodded, and Walt said, "Too many wives per man. What the hell would a man want with more than one, or even one, come to that?"

Higgins had an answer, but he asked, "Hungry yet, you boys? I'm gant."

He got up and went to his horse and took the deer from it. He laid out the carcass, then tied his horse to a tree, using a long rope so it could graze. The men were busy with their own horses. He took out the liver, peeled enough of the hide back to get out some good meat, then cut three roasting sticks. As the men returned, he asked, "Kick up the fire some, will you?"

"What I miss most," Dan said while they ate, "is a chair to sit on. Just a chair."

"Takes a spell to get used to the ground and your ham bones," Higgins told him.

They sat back and lighted pipes and listened to the night until Walt said, "Makes you think. All the people on the move, east to west. They'll be coming by saddle horse and wagon and — I wouldn't be surprised — afoot. Some women but mostly men."

"No wonder," Dan put in. "The way we heard it, it's just like you shoveled gold out of the stream beds."

"We're way early," Dan said. "But even so we passed a few outfits."

"Most of 'em takin' the shortcut?" Higgins asked.

"No. Not what we heard. Too tough was the word. It's Fort Bridger for them."

"Fact is," Walt added, "we passed just one outfit that was meaning to take it."

"Meaning, but not too likely to cut the mustard."

"I hope not."

Higgins asked, just to pass the time, "Ramshackle, huh?"

"Kind of," Dan answered. "Four men, one open wagon and seven horses. And did that wagon stink? One man said they had been killing buffalo for their hides but gave it up when they heard about California and gold. He was more or less friendly, not like the boss man, or the one we figured was boss."

Walt took up the talk. "There were just three saddle horses out of the seven. The others were draught stock. What they wanted with the wagon is more than I know. Just some shovels and bedrolls in it."

"What was holdin' 'em up?" Higgins asked.

"One man had taken sick, cramps and all. Besides, the wagon needed fixing. Loose tires for one thing. The delay didn't set well with the boss."

"Couldn't expect it to," Higgins said. He refilled and lit his pipe. It was pleasant enough just to palaver.

"The boss was one big son of a bitch," Walt said after a while. "Mean, too, it seemed like. Wouldn't you say so, Dan?"

"I wouldn't want to tangle with him. Worth your life to get a word out of him. Not like most travelers."

"Name of Cowgill or Crusoe, or something like that, the friendly one told us."

Higgins put off asking more. He didn't want to hear it. His mouth said, "Could it be Caudill?" He felt a small pinch in his guts. He hoped the answer was no.

"I do believe it might be. Know him?"

"Heard of him is all. Heard of a Boone Caudill."

"That's the man, then. What did you hear?"

"Only that he was a mountain man onct. You know, a beaver trapper. You say he's comin' by way of the shortcut."

"Yep."

"How close to here?"

"Three or four days, by our count."

"That's if the man gets over the cramps."

"What's a cramp or two to that boss?"

"Four days, I bet, figuring cramps and wagon trouble."

So, Higgins thought, it had poked down to the quick. Summers and Caudill, and Caudill close by at last. Jesus, with a whole world to traipse in, they were this close together. And he had to decide. Tell Summers or not? Just forget? Keep a secret from his best friend, thinking to spare him? A damn shaky excuse for the lie it would be. Tell him and let the chips fly?

Whatever he did, he better be where he could do it, he thought, feeling his mind was already halfway made up. If it wasn't, no harm in being on hand.

He got up of a sudden. "Keep the deer meat," he said to the men. "I got to go."

They looked surprised. Dan asked, "What's your hurry?"

"No hurry. It's just that time slips up on a man."

"You going to ride in the dark?" Walt asked.

"Moon's comin' up." He walked to his horse, untied it, tightened the cinch and got on. "Bye, men."

The moon had edged up, big as a platter, red as war paint, before he had gone far. He hummed to while away time and forget the miles ahead.

> Step and step and step, old hoss,
> We got a ways to go.
> Grass and grass for you, old hoss,
> We got a ways to go.
> Little Wing for me, old hoss,
> We got a ways to go.
> Step and —

He had been measuring his time to the pace of the horse. Now it struck him that he was making up words to a nowadays song.

> It's me, it's me, it's me, O Lord,
> Standin' in the need of prayer.

No special quarrel there. It stood to reason that everybody was in need of prayer, if so be it there were answers.

When the night was half gone, he watered the horse and let it graze for an hour. Then he swung back in the saddle. He rode out the night and the next day and came to camp along about sunset. Kettles were boiling. Little Wing ran out to welcome him. She said, looking at him, "You tired. You so tired. I take your horse." He let her, he was fagged, fagged and hungry, too.

They shared the fire and the food with Summers and his three. He talked talk for talk's sake until the meal was eaten and the women started cleaning up. He drew Summers aside then. They sat where the women wouldn't hear them.

"They found gold in Californy, Dick, a heap of it so I heerd, and a passel of people are movin' that way."

"Let 'em move. Let 'em stay. It don't hurt us."

. "I don't reckon so unless they branch out. All kinds of people on the move. All kinds."

"Gold would draw 'em."

"I reckon there won't be much hide-huntin' for a while."

"So?" Summers' keen gray eyes fastened on him. A man could feel them in the dusk. "What you tryin' to tell me, Hig?"

"Nothin' much." But Higgins knew it was no use. Trying to fool Summers, trying to lead him on by talking roundabout, was no use. He asked, "Anything eatin' on you, anything like before?"

"That's the drift, huh? I been tryin' to forget it. Go on. Somethin's eatin' on you."

"Secrets got a place in the world, I reckon."

"Depends."

"You won't do nothin' rash. Promise me that."

"Out with it, damn it. You know I ain't a headlong man."

"I located Boone Caudill, him you wanted to see."

"Where at?" Summers' voice had a snap in it.

"Him and three men are takin' the shortcut, bound for California."

"There now?"

"Be there in three or four days. Four most likely. But I used up a night and a day gettin' back."

Summers was silent for a long minute. Then he said, "It was meant all along. It was like it was writ in some book."

"What?"

"That him and me would meet up. I gave up lookin' for him. Put him almost out of my head. It ain't no accident, Hig. It's on purpose."

"Whose?"

"How do I know? It's just there."

"Shit. Be sensible. It's make-believe."

"Nope, Hig. Not when you hear the all of it. Comin' away from Oregon, before I teamed up with you, a man name of Birdwhistle sat by my fire. He had trapped and hunted with

Caudill. No mistakin' that. Call our meetin' just a stray hap-
penin' if you want to. But then I come onto Teal Eye. She was
Caudill's woman onct and had the boy by him. Then, like you
know, there was the talk at Fort Benton. Then come a blank,
but now you're tellin' me Caudill's comin' our way, just when
I was thinkin' no use dwellin' on him. So it ain't an accident.
Some things, seems like, was just meant to be, and no man can
whoa 'em."

"You aim to see him, then?"

"Got to." Summers rose. "Sunup."

26

SUMMERS set out at the first streaks of dawn, carrying what he might need in his saddle bags. His Hawken he held crosswise before him. He had some powder and ball. He always had that.

In his ears was Teal Eye's voice, speaking last night after he'd told her about Caudill. She had grasped his arm hard and said, "He kill you. He kill you."

"It ain't a killin' matter, little duck," he told her. "And it ain't so much I want to rub his nose in what he done. I just aim to set things straight. I been named to do it."

She shook him and cried out, "You have to, you kill him then. You are my man. Kill him."

"Like I said, it ain't a killin' matter. I talk straight, I leave."

But he wondered now how much truth he had told her.

There was no counting on Caudill to take things mild. He was a flare-up man, or had been in the old days.

In the old days, and Caudill and Jim Deakins on board the keelboat, both untried pups, and he had taken to them, no telling why, and tried to teach them what he knew. Later he had trapped with them and seen danger and gone with them to rendezvous, where Caudill with his strength had killed a man over nothing much. Caudill, brave and violent both, touchy as a sleeping dog, and Jim Deakins, a sunny boy who used his head, as unlike Caudill as a man could think.

But seasons softened old hard edges, and the days remembered swam before him, days of danger, fun and fight, all floating in a dream.

It struck him that he had become like Caudill in one way. He didn't like people messing around. He wanted what was leaving him, a world open and free, and his foot the first foot ever planted on a game trail, the first dipped in mountain water. A man walked with God then, or could think he did. There was a difference, though. Caudill hated people, hated settlements and laws. There was no flex in him. A man could like people but dislike crowds. He could like people but swear at what they did. He could accept law if not cotton to it. That, he thought, was him, Dick Summers, who felt bad at what was bound to happen and was happening to his world.

When night fell, he watered his horse and staked it out and, out of habit, built a small fire. A fire was good for more than heat and kettle. Sleep wouldn't be easy, not this night.

He ate and lit his pipe and saw the moon lifting and heard the footsteps of a horse. "Damn you, Hig," he said without turning, "I asked you to stay put. I told you never mind."

"Expectin' me, huh?"

"Expectin' but hopin' not." Higgins had reined in his horse. Its eyes caught a flicker from the fire. "Wisht you would foller orders."

"Orders? You know, I come twenty-one quite a while back,

and it's a free country, I been told. There's a bottle I been savin'. Might cure you of the sours. Got two grouse, too. Hold on while I mind my horse."

When he returned, he carried a bottle and two plucked grouse and said, "It ain't a jug but it's full. Might I please sit by the fire and offer you a drink?"

"You damn fool."

"You sure it's me?"

They drank and listened to the silence, broken only by moving water and a far-off coyote cry.

Into the silence Higgins said, "He's got men with him. Didn't seem a good fix, you against the four of them."

"Like I told Teal Eye, it won't come to that. I aim to tell him straight. It ain't right, Hig, for a man to carry wrong notions and maybe use them hurtful. Once he knows, he might feel sorry."

"That's your idea, to make him sorry?"

"Part of it, I reckon. A man who can't say he's sorry ain't fit company for anyone. But that's a side trail."

"What's really wormin' at you is Deakins got rubbed out and no good reason for it. You can't change that."

"I don't know what I can do, but I got to do it."

"You're a mule-minded man, Dick."

"Not my reputation."

"You're winnin' it."

For a while they sat quiet. Summers looked from the fire to the rising moon. The creek and the shore were silver, and shadows lay among the trees. Summers reached for a twig to light his pipe with. He puffed and said, "I'd like to set things straight."

"You and God, only God ain't so damn persnickety."

"I wouldn't be goin' except things came and came again. Somethin' out of sight and mind, some push I don't know the name of or the why for. Call it some big medicine, like the Indians. It keeps movin' me along. I speak out, then rest easy."

"If you get the chance."

"You can't say I'm wrong."

"I could but what's the use? Fate is what you're speakin' of, I reckon. I learned that word from a preacher, sayin' the fate of sinners was to go to hell."

"Fate it is, then. Please to pass the bottle."

They slept and woke up early and ate toasted grouse for breakfast and rode on. They reached the end of the cutoff before dark. Nothing moved along that trail, no horses, men or prairie schooners. There were hoof prints on the shore and wagon tracks up higher, and the char of dead fires.

"Too late, you reckon?" Summers asked.

"Them wagon tracks was here before. I figure we're on time."

Higgins went to picket the horses and came back saying, "No fool hens for our supper."

They built a fire and had a drink and ate jerky. Then they slept.

Not until the sun was high was there movement on the cutoff. Then three men and a pack train came angling down the slope. The horses whinnied and began lunging at the smell of water. The pack train broke loose and came on, followed by the riders. The horses plunged their noses in the river. The men fell from their saddles and bellied down.

Summers yelled out, "Easy on the water! Small doses else you'll puke."

One man lifted up, his chin dribbling. "Christ, it's good."

"A little at a time."

The man got to his feet and shook the others, saying, "Stop it now. You know better."

The other two men drew back from the shore. One of them said, "Lucky to be alive." His eyes went to Summers. "We started late and in the dark strayed off the trail and made the driest damn camp ever known."

"Moon up and all?" Summers asked, letting his voice be dry.

"Strangers in a strange land," the first man said. "Easier from here on, or do you know?"

"Better'n what you just come over," Summers told him. "Take my word."

The men drank again. One of them belched. Another walked out to keep the horses close. The third one said, "We're pushin' on directly. First come, first served in California." He said to Summers, "Could I ask what's keeping you, mister?"

"Waitin' for friends. You pass anybody?"

"It's way early for the most of them, and those we saw were going Bridger way."

"No one on the cutoff?"

"Just one outfit. A wagon, open, and four men."

"Might be our friends. How far behind you?"

"The way they were going, I'd say three or four hours."

The men got back in their saddles and reined north, along the trail proper. They waved as they went, and Summers called, "Good luck."

Higgins left him, and he heard two shots, and Higgins came back with one rabbit and one grouse. They weren't much for two hungry stomachs.

They sat through the blazing afternoon in what shade they could find, their eyes fixed on the cutoff. Little heat waves danced there to the sun's tune. A breeze stirred and died.

At last Summers said, "Someone's comin', Hig."

"Wisht I had your eyes."

They waited.

A wagon came lurching down the hill, held back with ropes that three men pulled while the fourth yanked at the team. Summers said, "Light load, else they couldn't hold 'er. There's Caudill."

Horses, wagon, men picked up their pace with water just ahead. They made a line along the shore. The men got up, wiping their mouths. From twenty feet away Summers called, "How, Boone?"

Caudill came forward, scowling. The years had coarsened him, and time laid on some fat, but muscles played beneath it. The scowl disappeared. "Hang me if it ain't Dick Summers. How?" He held out his hand. Summers let himself shake.

"What goes with you? Where's your stick float?" Caudill asked.

"It's a long story."

"Come with us, along to Californy, you and your ganted-up friend."

"Don't be belittlin' him, Boone."

"All right. Come along."

"Don't reckon so. Let's talk a spell." Summers made for a dead and drifted log and beckoned Caudill. Caudill yelled to his men, "See to the horses. Make camp. Me and an old friend got to jabber."

"How come the wagon?" Summers asked.

"Two of my pardners ain't worth a shit on a horse, and the wagon might come in handy. The men can shovel, by God. They'll shovel when we get to pay dirt."

"Heard you were huntin' hides?"

"A man's got to live. What's with you, I done asked once?"

"I'm a settled man, married and everything."

"You mean really married? By a preacher?"

It was time to let him have it, or some of it. "Yep," he said. "Me and Teal Eye."

Caudill jerked his head to stare at Summers. "Teal Eye? My old squaw?"

"She ain't old. Your boy's growin' up."

"Not my boy, by God. You watch out, she'll cheat on you."

"She never cheated on anybody."

"Like hell you say. Birthed a boy with red hair like Jim Deakins. A blind pup to boot."

"You ever see a white buffalo?"

"One time."

"Could you pick out his pa?"

"You talk crazy talk."

"Trouble with you, Boone, you never knew what real friendship was."

"You speakin' of Jim Deakins, I saved his life onct."

"And took it for nothin' at all, nothin' but what you made up in your mind."

Caudill's face was full-turned to him with such a look of torment in it that Summers felt minded to say, "Now, Boone. Easy. It ain't the first mistake ever made." But the look of torment changed to black rage.

Summers, with his hand on his knife, thought he was prepared. He wasn't, not for the heavy arm flung across his chest. It knocked him backward over the log. Caudill rolled over and straddled him. He locked his strong hands on his throat.

Summers had his knife out. He couldn't slash at the arms or hands, not with his upper arm pinned by the great weight of the knee. The forearm was free with the knife in it. He could jab it into a gut. He didn't, not yet. The hands clamped tighter. His lungs churned for air. But even as his sight dimmed and his senses blurred, he kept the knife by his side. It wasn't a killing matter.

He thought he heard the crack of a rifle. He thought he felt the big body lurch and then tremble. Then most of it fell forward at his side. He squirmed out from under. There was a hole in Caudill's head just under the hairline.

Panting, he looked up. Higgins stood a few feet away, a wisp of smoke drifting from the muzzle of his Kentucky.

Higgins said, "He didn't mean nothin' to me."

Summers couldn't answer for the clench of fingers still felt on his windpipe.

Higgins turned to the watching men. There he was, seen dimly, a skinny rack of bones unarmed except for the unloaded rifle. "You want to make something of it?" he asked.

One of the men answered, "It ain't no skin off our ass."

"Get shovels, then. We got to dig a grave. I'll help."

The same man said, "Be a pleasure."

Summers just sat, his hand lying on Caudill's dead shoulder. He sat and watched the men and the hole growing deeper. He tried not to think, tried not to remember how it was long ago.

He patted the shoulder and got up and walked to the men. "Time," he said and tried to clear the squeeze from his voice. "Time to be goin' home."

Part Three

◆

27

SUMMERS sat by the shore of the Teton and watched the water flow by. He had a pole in his hand and a baited hook in the water, but the hook had washed into the shallows and he let it ride there. Below him near the tepees, almost out of earshot, were Teal Eye and the boys and Higgins and Little Wing, talking a mixture of Shoshone, Blackfoot and English. They sounded happy.

A log cabin sat by the tepees now, built by him and Higgins because the womenfolk seemed to want one. It was chinked with clay and had a tramped-earth floor, a sod roof and two real-glass windows packed in from Fort Benton. In hot weather it was cooler than the tepees, and in windy weather it was better for cooking because of a mud-and-stick fireplace that didn't smoke. Not so good in cold weather, though. Nothing like a tepee for warmth. It had gone a little against the grain to build it. It seemed too solid, too much there forever, as if it held them to one spot. Still?

The older a man got, he thought, the more he liked just to sit and watch water run. The Teton was a hurrying stream, as if it couldn't wait to join up with the Marias and empty into the Missouri and go on and on just for the fun of running and joining. It was a young buck, full of frolic and fizz, eager for the yonders, its clean flow muddied, and would wind up in big and mixed waters that lazed along to the sea.

A trout rose, but he didn't cast for it. Enough to sit here and look while the soft summer afternoon inched along. A spiky bunch of flowers made patches of yellow on the far shore, and johnny-jump-ups grew in the moist soil near his feet. He picked one and smelled it and chewed at the stem.

The Teton, it was mostly called now, though it had borne and bore different names, given it by explorers, trappers, stray visitors and traveling preachers and priests. Names like the Tansy, the Rose and the Breast, which was just English for Teton, meaning the breast of a woman to Frenchmen. Those Frenchies, good with a boat but not worth a damn fighting Indians, the Frenchies, coming up the Missouri or boating and hauling by way of Canada, and all of them starved for women, so that every nippled butte put them in mind of a tit, and every swell of land might be the swell of she flesh. If he got up and looked back, he could see a butte like that and the swell of land leading to it.

Wherever he was, whatever was in his head, worry about the boys kept sneaking in. Lives flowed just as rivers did. But how? And to where? What would happen to Nocansee without him and Teal Eye around? He had grown big and strong like his blood father, but not like him in anything else. He was a gentle boy, a good, soft-hearted boy, with senses so sharpened that a man wondered. He had a nose keen as a hound's, ears that picked up what other ears couldn't, and such a feeling for touch that he seldom stumbled or fell. But what good were they without eyes to see? No answer to that one.

And no ready answer for Lije. How to shoot, how to hunt, how to trail or lie patient, how to read footprints, how to learn from the wind and the voices of birds — what good in the life he would have to lead as the world changed? It wasn't enough that he had a brain and was able of body. It wasn't enough that he knew a little of numbers and letters. Somehow he would have to learn more in the coming time of account books and ledgers and buying and selling and the ways and the tricks of business. He must learn how to read and to write.

It was hard to believe, the years flowed so fast, that Nocansee was nineteen or thereabouts, and Lije a coming sixteen.

He sighed and put worry in the back of his head. The sun was good on his back. Under it the fields to the east and the far bank of the valley shone soft and green-yellow. A man might almost think they were smiling. To his right, maybe five miles away, two craggy buttes lifted, good enough to the eye to excuse the presence of rattlesnakes. On their slopes antelopes would be feeding, curious as cats, slender-legged, their rumps showing white when they turned.

He had put worry in the back of his head except for one niggle. That was Higgins. He hadn't seemed quite himself lately, pretty quiet these days as if some secret worked in him. A man with wife trouble might act and look like that. Not likely with Little Wing. But who could tell?

Such worries aside, it was a good life he was leading, good in spite of hard winters and winds that beat a man backward, good though travelers, Indian and white, rode up and down and across the valley as they hadn't before. The Indians were no problem. They shied off from the camp or came to visit polite, remembering tales of Bear Friend and Bear Maker. The whites scouted the land and went on, to where gold might be found or to the eastern plains where the great herds of buffalo roamed. Gold-hunter and hide-hunter, and nothing much for either one of them here, nothing much for anybody except those who felt kin to mountains and flats and liked to see distance too far to figure.

The past spring had seen a big party of whites, though — men, wagons, teams and tackle — and some men sighted through instruments and others held poles, and once in a while they planted a stake, and Summers knew them for surveyors. It was Blackfoot country, this country was, made so by treaty, but here was the advance party of whites getting ready to parcel it out.

They had gone on, leaving no signs of their passage except for a here-and-there marker, which Summers and Higgins tore from the ground when they came on them.

Moon after moon, Summers thought, watching the ripples and small sprays of water. Moon after moon since their return to the old camping grounds — springs, summers, falls, winters, each in its own manner and none quite the same as before, so that a man could speak of the season and year of the big flood, of the long drought, of the grandfather of winds. On a day like today he would laugh at the winters that kept all hands inside, except for bringing in more firewood or axing a chunk of meat off a carcass stowed outside just as the real cold set in. A lazy time then, but not lazy when a man could get out and had to hunt hard for meat, not lazy when furs were prime and he waded in water that withered the skin and made his legs blue.

He heard the soft crunch of grass and looked up, and Higgins asked, "Just settin', lazy bones?"

"Settin' and thinkin'."

"Don't fag your mind. Thinkin' on what?"

Summers motioned toward the ground. "Have a seat. My mind's on my boys."

"Bein' a pa puts a weight on a man, on a man like you leastwise. All the same, I wisht Little Wing and me could come up with a baby."

Summers let his gaze follow the river, down to the curve that it made. "Growed up, what would he do, Hig? Not live like us, that's for sure. You think this valley's goin' to stay like it is? Some galoot with a plow will come along, or some bastard will think, Jesus what a country for beef cattle now that the buffalo's gone. You know there's cattle already down on the Medicine and over on the Gallatin, too."

"Seems a shame, though, that a man with a good wife has no young'n to show for it. If it was different, I bet me and her would have a world-beater or somethin' close to it."

So there was no trouble between Higgins and Little Wing. It had been foolish to wonder.

Summers went on, still thinking of the baby Higgins wished for. "You seen them surveyors, Hig. It's notice of where at we're headed. We've both been to Fort Benton, recent enough to know what it is. It's not just a fort anymore. It's a stinkin' town. Boats on the river, freight comin' in, freight goin' out, mine tackle and such for the west, buffalo hides for the east. Beggin' Indians, drunk Indians, made that way by the whites who hate 'em. But, hell, you know."

"No harm in wishin'," Higgins said. "You talk true enough, but a man goes crazy if he tries to figure all the ins and outs and whatever will come after he's dead. Besides, Little Wing she wants a baby."

Summers gave him a smile and said, "Thanks from your crazy friend."

No trouble between Higgins and Little Wing, and a man couldn't call it husband-and-wife trouble between him and Teal Eye. It was the difference between facing facts and balking at doing it. They were lying together at night, and he had asked, "What you reckon is ahead for Lije?"

"He will take a wife, not so long now."

"I don't want him to be a fort loafer or to hang around at some Indian agency. I don't want him to turn out a drunk like so many."

"You have taught him better."

"It's a white man's world comin' up. Where does he fit?"

"He will live with us like always, his wife with him."

"I'm afraid that ain't likely."

"You mean he leaves us?"

"When the time comes. It has to be."

His arm across her felt the sudden spasm of grief. She began to cry without sound.

"I don't want him to leave, neither, little duck." He tried patting her shoulder. "It's just that what's what is what. What is bound to be will be."

She didn't answer.

"If I see straight, the old life's about over. No matter if I don't like it, new times are comin'. I want him ready."

"You talk like a white man." Her shoulder pulled away from his hand.

"I've growed to be more Indian than white," he told her. "The country's done it, you and the country and all. A man gets shaped to what is around him. If I talk like a white man, it's because I was one onct, and I know 'em."

She didn't speak again, but he knew it was grief, not dislike, that had silenced her. Nothing like a hard fact to jar up a couple.

Now Higgins said, "You do a heap of thinkin', if that's what you're doin'."

Before Summers could answer, they heard the bray of a mule.

"I be damned," Higgins said, getting up fast.

Summers came to his feet, too. "Round the bend. Beyond them trees. Come on."

"With nothin' in hand except a fish pole."

"I'll take it. We're fishin'."

They rounded the bend, stepping soft, and saw two men, two horses and a pack mule. One of the men was out from shore, washing gravel in a pan. The other, on the bank, was white-whiskered and wore a pistol on his hip. Seeing them, he made out to draw it until Summers asked, "Any luck?"

"If we had any, you think we'd tell you?"

"Likely not, but without luck maybe so you would. Me and my pardner gave it up and turned to fishin'. My name's Summers. This here is Higgins."

"Ralston," the man said and offered his hand. "Him haulin' ass out of the creek is named Tevis. You say you done panned this water?"

"Sure did. Both forks. From headwaters clean to the Marias and never found a show."

Tevis came up, pants dripping, a shovel and a pan in his hand. He shook his head. "No good. No fuckin' good."

"What with diggin' and washin' and watchin' for Indians, we got a bellyful," Ralston said.

Higgins said, "With that hee-haw horse singin' a come-on, I'd watch sharp for redskins."

"Any around here, close, I mean?" Ralston asked.

"Some. They come and they go," Summers answered.

"They on the peck?"

"It depends. They get some upset when the whites mine their gold or kill off their buffalo."

Tevis dropped bucket and pan and stepped ahead. "You sayin' it's theirs?"

The man was too damn much. Summers said, "I'm sayin' they're sayin' it's theirs, and I'm sayin' it could be. You want to get your dander up, do it."

"Now, now," Ralston said. "No offense anywhere. The point is, Indians and troubles. You had any?"

"Not to speak of. We both of us got Indian wives."

"Sweet Jesus," Tevis said and spit on the ground. "Get the mule, Ralston."

As they rode away, Tevis said, just loud enough for them to hear, "Squawmen."

"A man could wish they get their scalps lifted," Summers told Higgins. "Gold. By-God gold."

Higgins scuffed at the ground with the toe of one moccasin. "Somethin' I been meanin' to bring up, Dick." He sat down, saying, "Set a minute."

Summers sat, holding the fish pole upright, the hook set in the butt. "I knowed you had some burr under your tail."

"All right. It's money. It's gold. We got to get some."

"What for?"

"You damn well know. To pay debts. They bear hard on a man."

"I'm mindful."

"There ain't enough fine furs, you can't catch enough, me helpin', to pay what we owe at Fort Benton. It's a right smart of money, what with new horses and all."

"So?"

"You got the three new ones on jawbone, sayin' you'd pay later, but, knowin' you, I know you was embarrassed down to the bone."

Summers flicked the end of the fish pole at a leaf overhead. "You don't need to tell me we're owin'. I got the figure in my head. And I can trap enough furs, come the time that they're prime. Don't forget, the money ain't due yet. You ever know me to back out on a debt?"

"There's another thing it's in me to tell you."

"Spit it out."

"It's what I owe you, and only one way I can see to pay it."

"You don't owe me nothin'."

"Like hell. I ain't mentioned it till now, but it's been ridin' in my mind ever since we met up. Long as you had some money and we added a mite with our traps, I just floated along, all the time feelin' obliged but not pushed. Now you're broke, flat broke, and I ain't floatin' no more. Been too goddamn long as it is. High time to pay up."

Summers put the pole down and looked into Higgins' eyes. They were stubborn. "You're my pardner, Hig."

"Some pardner. More like beggin' kin. That money you

earned guidin' to Oregon, that gold coin, you paid it out from the very beginnin', and then put up for my wife. That busted you good."

"Push it out of your mind for Christ's sake."

"Nope. Gone too far and too long, things have. You got your honor as I damn well know, so give me mine. I'm goin' to where the gold is, Bannack or more likely that new strike they call Alder Gulch, somewhere where there's gold."

"I'll loan you a shovel."

"Don't try to put me off, makin' fun. My mind's made up. Them places ain't so far away."

"I'm too old to muck around heavin' gravel."

"Bullshit. Where gold is, there's a good chance of gettin' some without minin'."

"I never set up as a gambler, crooked or straight."

Higgins rose and started walking away. "I mean to go, Dick." He glanced back. "With you or without you. Think on it."

28

IT WAS A COUNTRY of sweeping valleys they had come through, of sweeping valleys and Christly high hills, mostly bald, with one now and then fringed near the top or patched higher up with dwarf pine or brush. A man was put in mind of giant heads that had lost most of their hair.

The trip rolled through Higgins' head. Up the Missouri to the Three Forks, up the Madison, with Summers leading like a hound on a scent. "I can sure as hell find the Three Forks and the Madison," he had said, "and where there's water there's game trails and pony tracks likely and the marks of travois. It's white man's pride says we discovered this country. The Indians knowed it before."

At the Three Forks he had told them, "It was around here that Immel and Jones and their men got rubbed out. Blackfeet."

But they had seen little of Indians — a couple of hunting parties and one camp — and these had given no trouble.

Valleys and hills that were trying to be mountains and might brag of a timberline if they kept growing, say for two hundred years. River and creek crossings, go-rounds where gorges choked travel, buffalo here, buffalo there, antelopes watching, the sun high and hot and low and cooled down, and pitch camp and break camp for another hard day after short sleep. Summers in the lead, trailing two pack horses, the women mounted, Lije on his own horse leading another that Nocansee sat on and himself at the tail end with two more pack horses in tow.

Higgins watched while the horses drank. Here was Alder Gulch. Here was the creek muddied by pans and sluice boxes. Up and down and in the stream were men working, their eyes fixed on what shovels brought up and water cleared. No time for how-de-do and a chat. No time but for searches and grunts and a glad yelp once in a while. So far as his eyes could see, side to side, were nothing but claims and the men working them.

Summers had found the place, not asking questions, going by what he knew from before, going by hunch or some secret sense like a migrating loon. So it was up Grasshopper Creek and on to Bannack, which seemed to be dying out and then on the traveled road to Alder Gulch. He had picked a camp site on a hillside northeast of the settlement where a trickle of water flowed, enough just about to cook by. Later in the season it would dry up.

He let the horses drink their fill. Likely they would be dropping mud balls by morning. So be it. No harm done. No harm in letting the mind run far and high, seeing the valleys and hills again and the Madison where trout asked to be caught.

The tepees were up and a fire burning when he got back to their camping place, puffing from the climb. Summers had built a rock and earth dam to catch the little water that seeped close by. Higgins hobbled the horses except for three that they trusted not to range far. He put a bell on one that they didn't, hobbles or no. Afterward he said to Summers, "Christ, Dick, there's miners clear up and down the gulch, miles of 'em, and what town I seen was tents and wood shacks a breeze would blow down, all strung along in the dirt."

"It follers."

They stood, toeing the ground now and then, waiting for supper. The boys were close up, silent and listening.

"I reckon their eyes have turned yeller," Higgins said.

"Gold-eyed. That's what they come for. That's us, too."

"It's what I aim to get."

Into a little silence Nocansee said, "Someone comes."

From a dip in the side of the hill two horsemen appeared, heads showing first, then shoulders, and horses and all of them as they climbed. By and by they could make the men out, their faces bearded like an old buffalo bull's, their pants and shirts stained, their boots crusted with mud. They pulled their horses to a stop. "We figured there might be a stream flowin' down this here coulee. You stakin' a claim?"

"Naw," Summers answered. "Not us. There's the stream you was lookin' for, flowin' drop by drop. We tried a pan or two just for luck. No color. Stake if you want to. Minin's not our business."

The men studied the tepees and eyed the women and boys who stood near, and the second one said, "It don't look like it for a fact."

The first one said, "I don't guess it's any use."

"I say go up the gulch, way up where no son of a bitch is. No tellin' how far the strike runs. Come on."

They rode away.

Once they had eaten, Higgins told Summers, "Reckon I'll mosey down into town. Might pay to scout around. Comin'?"

"Teal Eye, Lije," Summers said, turning, "we're leavin' for a spell. I figure the camp will be safe enough, but remember you got the scattergun and the musket. Load 'em but don't use 'em careless."

Teal Eye smiled and said for a joke, "We play with them. Throw around. Make big noise."

"I shoot straight, too," Little Wing put in.

"Hell, Dick," Higgins said, "you got so used to carryin' a rifle you feel naked without it. I say leave our shootin' irons. What good they do us?"

"None to my knowin'."

Along the gulch lights were showing as the dusk settled, and voices sounded and the frail music of strings. They walked down the rough street, looking and listening. Men traipsed back and forth, going from one saloon to another, from one gambling table, Higgins guessed, to another where luck might be better. They spoke loud. Their voices rose and were lost in the great silence around them, lost in the sky and among the hills where they were no matter. If a man wanted to learn to cuss, here was the school for it.

"My fiddle sounds better than that there hurdy-gurdy," Higgins said.

"And tepees are better'n tents."

A good part of the camp was tents, staked to the ground or to wood platforms. Some places were part tent and part wood. The best were built of poles or logs or whipsawed lumber, and a man could throw a cat through the cracks. The best one, a saloon, had a plank walk in front of it.

A freight string of mules — eight mules, four yoke Higgins counted — had pulled in, and men were unloading boxes and barrels and such from the five wagons they'd drawn. The men cussed because the delivery was late, and the driver cussed back at them. They worked in shadow. The best of lamps didn't throw out much light.

Two men broke out of a saloon door, their speech loud and hard-edged. "By God we'll settle this," one of them said.

"Try it, you Yank son of a bitch!"

They squared off, but the talk wasn't quite over. "Talk about me, you're a goddamn galvanized Yank."

"I done fit for my side, and that's more than you ever done. Hurrah for Jeff Davis."

"My ass to him. Hurrah for the union."

Jeff Davis swung and Union went down. He got up, his mouth bleeding, and said, "We'll beat you bastards." But the fight had gone out of him. He went back into the saloon.

Summers said, "Friend, not my business but seems you got your differences."

"Whose side you on?"

Higgins answered for Summers. "I don't guess we rightly know. Got to hear more of the fors and againsts."

"Where the hell you been? In a hole? Don't you know the country's at war, south against north?"

Summers said, "Sure. Even where we was we picked up some things. But it's a far piece away and come to us like an echo. Slaves or no slaves, that's the stickin' point, way we heerd."

"You could say it started there, I s'pose, but now the south's broken off from the union."

"We heerd that, too."

"That's our right, ain't it? To secede? We got our own president and officers and way of livin'. Don't tell me that's not our right."

"Not tellin' you anything," Summers said. "How's the war comin'?"

"You can't tell, not out here. Seesaw, I would say. I was took prisoner early and to get out of that stinkin' prison I promised not to fight anymore."

"Looks like you done busted that promise," Higgins said.

"Not to fight in the army, I promised. They call them like me galvanized Yanks."

"This camp's split, huh?" Summers asked.

"Split all to hell. It's gold that holds it together. I got a good-payin' claim my own self. Buy you a drink?"

"Obliged, but I reckon not. No offense and glad to hear your side of it. Too bad, though, Americans fightin' Americans."

The man nodded, unoffended. "It's them union, abolitionist bastards forced us to it."

He went off for the drink he had mentioned.

"I swear, it looks like we don't know nothin' much," Higgins said. "A big war, and us only hearin' the littles of it."

"Just so it don't reach out to us. Men fight and die and both sides dead right to their thinkin', and a man lookin' square at things can't make up his mind. Only sure thing is that the side that loses is more'n ever set in its notions."

They lazed on until a man in a black business suit stopped them. He had a trimmed beard and looked like a Dutchman Higgins once knew.

Looking at Summers in his buckskins, he asked, "You be a hunter, yah?"

"I been known to shoot."

The man gave his name, but Higgins couldn't catch all of it. It was Con something or other.

"I have butcher shop," the man went on. "Sell meat, you know." He shook his head. "Meat. Sometimes I get the old ox, up from the Oregon Trail. Sometimes I get longhorns, and the meat be as tough as the horn. No good, but I sell it."

Summers nodded.

"If I get deer, if I get elk, maybe buffalo, I pay good."

Summers said, " 'Pears to me this country's pretty well hunted out, or scared out."

"Not so. Nobody hunts but for gold. A good hunter find plenty."

"Maybe."

"I pay twenty-five dollars in good dust for a deer, forty for an elk, and for a buffalo — " He spread his hands wide.

"Antelope?"

"Fifteen for that little meat. You bring them in, gutted is all, and I give you gold, fair weight, on the spot."

"I might short you on deer liver."

"All right. All right. You hunt for me?"

"I'll give it a try. Name's Dick Summers."

Con wrung Summers' hand before he walked on.

"Hard work, this job-huntin'," Higgins said.

"We maybe can do all right."

"Figure me out, Dick. I got an idee of my own." He wasn't ready to say what his idea was — to sing and play for the miners, who might feel like putting a little something in his hat.

29

SUMMERS called out, "Meat. Here's your meat."

He had pulled up in back of the butcher shop. His pack horses carried two deer and one elk, canvas-wrapped against the flies. A couple of curious men and three dogs had followed him at some distance.

The butcher came out of the shop. He said, "By Gott, what you have?"

"Two deer, one elk. Meat's still sweet."

It was. He hadn't given it time to sour, and now he felt on him the drag of the long ride. "Hard huntin'," he said as he slid from his horse.

The butcher was working with the canvases. Summers went to help him, standing his rifle against the back of the building.

The butcher, his apron bloodier than when he came out, said,

"Meat not shot up, by Gott." He was looking at the two deer carcasses, now unwrapped.

"One hole is all."

The man's eyes went from the deer, to Summers, to the standing rifle. "That old iron shoot goot, yah?"

"Good enough."

"Goot for the goot eye." The man smiled. He kicked at a dog that had come too close.

The two curious men now stood near. One of them said, "I can't believe my damn eyes, Con. Fresh meat and tender to boot. Last chunk you sold me bounced my jaw out of place. Save me a piece, will you?"

"How much?"

"Say five pounds. How much you chargin'?"

The butcher shrugged. "How I know so soon? It be a bargain."

The second man said, "Same for me, Con."

Con turned to Summers. "Must hurry. It all be sold before I cut it up."

A young man, a boy, had come out of the shop. The butcher turned on him. "Gott damn you, Hans. Help. What you do in there? Yust dream?"

The unwrapped carcasses lay on the canvases that had covered them. The butcher, helped a little by the boy, started skinning.

"You want me to, I can give you a hand," Summers said. Con clapped a hand to his forehead. It left a blotch of blood there.

"I forget, all the time forget. Pay you want now."

"Not for helpin'."

He got out his Green River knife. It was old but sharper than when it was new. Watching for a moment, Con said, "See, Hans. Learn, boy. This man be a skinner."

An hour later they carried the skinned meat inside, laying a deer carcass on a block. Summers washed his hands from a bucket of muddy water. The butcher wiped his on a soiled rag.

The butcher said, "I cut up for sale, but first I pay you."

They went into the front of the shop. It held another block and a rough counter and a gold scale. On the counter were a few scraps of meat turning black.

"Ninety dollars I make it. Yah?"

"That's right."

From his pocket Con took out a pouch and began pouring small nuggets and gold dust on the scale.

"Hold on," Summers said. "What do I carry it in?"

"You have not the poke, like this in my hand?"

"Never thought I'd need one."

"Everybody have one." The scales balanced, but Con added an extra pinch. "For good measure. You want me to keep, then? You trust me? Ask any man."

"I'll get it the next time."

"Goot. You keep me in meat, yes?"

"Fur as I can."

It had been a long way to meat and a long way back. On these open hills and wide valleys, game could spot a man a long way from the reach of a rifle. No trees to speak of and few watering places, so that wildlife was far-ranging and, knowing the ways of man, spooky. He had found a spring with a patch of growth on its borders and had lain there unmoving, while the sun came up and arched over and hid behind the hills. Flies buzzed around him, the damn deer flies that came straight on and bit before a body could slap, if he dared to slap while playing dead, and mosquitoes hummed for a landing place, their little needles ready for action. But deer came, as expected, and one elk, and the live deer took off after one shot and were out of range before he could reload, and then there was waiting again.

He felt his muscles hang slack, as if ready to drop off the bone, and he yawned as he turned away. Tomorrow he would rest. He led the horses to water and let them drink and then from his saddle pulled the string up the hill. They were tired, too, not so much from work as from standing and fighting the flies. Only mosquitoes bothered them now that the sun was about down.

Pretty soon the miners would be knocking off work and tramping the street, looking for excitement and maybe finding a fight in a bottle, or maybe taking the edge off, thanks to a whore. There were bound to be some, a few, about. There always were where men gathered. The lights down below were coming on, as feeble as candle gleams.

Teal Eye and Lije ran out to meet him. Seeing the bloody canvases, Teal Eye said, "Where is meat?"

"I done sold it."

"We go hungry then," she said, not as if really believing.

"Deer livers in my saddle bags. Good enough for you?"

She thumbed him in the ribs. "Me, I should know. Lije, you take the horses. Your papa tired."

Nocansee walked up, not stumbling, "How the big hunter? I smell deer and what — elk?"

"No keepin' secrets from you," Summers answered and tapped the boy's shoulder.

Higgins lounged up, trailed by his woman. "Trust you to bring home the bacon."

The women began taking the wrapped livers from the saddle bags, and Lije was lifting the gear from the horses.

"Man who brings home the bacon has a right to a drink," Higgins went on.

"Camp was dry, last time I seen it."

"They sell whiskey down in the big city. Makes a man wonder where's the most money, in mines or in barrels."

They sat and drank, taking it easy, while the women cooked.

"Made out pretty good, did you?" Higgins said.

"Ninety dollars' worth."

"I call that more'n fair."

"Hard-earned money."

Higgins drank. "I found out one thing. Gold or gold dust is

the only money passed hereabouts. So a man needs what they call a poke."

"I found that out already."

"What you don't know is the women made us one each, drawstrings and all. Better'n most, too, bein' beaded."

"The butcher's holdin' my dust for me."

"I'll have some to put in mine." Higgins' broken mouth smiled. "I got me a job."

"What? Good one?"

"Startin' tonight. You're so tired you ain't noticed how I was dandied up." Now Summers took note that his buckskins had been cleaned and brushed, his hair fresh-washed and braided and tied with ribbons.

"Where's the ball?"

"At first I thought I'd put out a felt hat, crown down, but dust wouldn't pour good from felt. It would stick and, first thing you know, someone would try pannin' the hat. So I'm takin' a tin cup."

"I'm beginnin' to track."

"The cup and my fiddle. I'm singin' for my supper."

"Where at?"

"That saloon with the boardwalk. It's called the Here's Howdy."

"You'll get sick, breathin' that air. It stinks."

"I can stand 'er, but I know. Spilled beer and whiskey. Men smellin' rank. And them shithouses. The Indians knowed better, scatterin' it around instead of pilin' it up."

"What's the pay?"

"Nothin'. Only what the boys want to put in the cup. I figure I can sing 'em open-handed. Worth a try, anyhow. Now I got to eat and be goin'."

The last Summers saw of him that night was the bony figure, fiddle and tin cup in hand, walking down the long grade toward the lights.

30

SUMMERS said to Teal Eye, "I'm oneasy in my mind."

They sat in the starshine outside the tepee. Nocansee was nearby, listening. He was a quiet boy — or man — and what went on in his head he didn't tell. Lije had gone to bed. Little Wing, likely hearing the talk, came up and sat down.

"He will be all right," Teal Eye answered.

"Like I told him, it's a tomfool thing, carryin' his poke around."

"He is proud of it like a little boy," Little Wing said. "Proud to have money. Proud because he can pay debt to you."

"That poke's a fair weight, comin' full."

"Yours, too," Teal Eye told him. "You brought in the big buffalo."

"I go armed. All Hig's got is his fiddle, his fiddle and that poke that somebody'll want. He thinks everyone loves him. But come a fight between love and gold, gold wins. That's what I tried to get into his head."

Little Wing said, "It is just this one more time he sings. He said it to all."

"That's just it." Summers scratched himself. More damn places itched. Far off a wolf howled, sounding lonesome as the last of the pack. The stars shone brighter and cleaner than the lights of the town.

"The night's gettin' on," he said. "You be all right if I traipse into town?"

"You know it," Teal Eye told him. "We call Lije. We have the scattergun and the musket, so all right. Be all right, too."

He picked up his rifle and started down the hill. A horse would get him there sooner, but he'd arrive soon enough. No one would tackle Hig while he played to a crowd.

The smell of the place reached him before he came to it. This was what men did, what bunches of men did — tear up and stink up a location and foul the water and leave the land wrecked when the gold ran out, leave the land torn and the water nasty until maybe at last God got around to mending things. No guarantee that he would.

The sounds of the voice and the fiddle floated through the open door of the saloon. Higgins was playing and singing some jig tune to the thumps of boots and whiskey yells. Summers poked his head inside. Men were dancing, alone and together, some with the scatter of whores who tried not to look too old for the business. Higgins had a little platform for himself.

Summers pulled his head back and snorted the stink out. The place smelled of beer, whiskey, dirt and sweat. Nice place for a picnic. The street, up and down, was deserted. Now was the time to drown the work of the day in a jug.

The music stopped, and hands clapped, and yells called for more.

Summers heard Higgins call out, "Ladies and gents, time to

cool off and get your breath back. Soothin' music it is now."

Out of his long-ago boyhood Summers remembered snatches of song. "Pretty Saro" was one, heard again over the gap of years. The crowd was silent except for one drunken voice. There was the sound of fist against flesh, and the voice died. There was another song and another, and yes, now there was "Barbara Allen." After each came hand clapping, boot stomping and shouts for still more. Then Higgins played what Summers knew was his own song.

> To me my ma weren't a lady.
> To me she was only plain Ma
> Who cooked the grits and the hog meat
> For me and a man known as Pa.
>
> He wasn't my pa, I can tell you.
> He caught Ma when she was lone
> And made out for sure that he loved her
> And then called our house his own.
>
> I hated his lights and his liver.
> I hated him kernel and shell,
> And I prayed the devil to take him
> Down to the furnace of hell.
>
> Then he met a slim filly named Lily
> Who nobody ever called shy,
> And took off with her for the city
> And left us to root hog or die.
>
> We made out, we made out, me and Ma did,
> Thanks to her grit and her head.
> Looking back, I cry in my whiskers,
> Wishing that Ma wasn't dead.
>
> Ma, oh, Ma, can you hear me?
> Your touch was so gentle and strong,
> I know now that you was a lady,
> But why did it take me so long?

There was silence when the song ended and then a sudden blast of hands, voices, stomping feet. In answer to it Higgins

played the last verse again and then again the last line, adding
to it and putting in more throb.

> But why did it take me so long, so long?
> Oh, why did it take me so long?

His voice sounded above the other noises. "Ladies and gents,
I thank you kindly. Now I'm sung out."

Summers waited, knowing that Higgins would sit there until the men had had a chance to sweeten the cup. Then he
would empty the cup into his poke and come out.

He looked up and down the street again. Now was a likely
time, and after a while, sure enough, two men came from in
back of a building. He eased himself into the shadows between
two shops. Higgins walked through the doorway and started
down the road, his fiddle in one hand, his poke swinging from
its thong in the other. The two men came close on his heels.
Summers sneaked up from behind.

One of the men said, "Turn around. Got a gun on you. Hand
over that poke."

"Oh, don't hurt me," Higgins whined, turning. "Here's the
poke." He swung it as he turned. It caught the man over the
temple. The man staggered and went down.

Hands apart on his Hawken, Summers swung it over the
other man's head and pulled the man to him. A squeak came
out of the choked throat. The man was small. He kicked like a
held rabbit.

"Get their pokes," Summers said.

Higgins collected them. "Not one hell of a lot in 'em."

"The pistol."

Higgins lifted it from where it had fallen. "It's no more'n a
toy. One shot if it fired at all." He tossed it into the street.

Summers let the little man drop. The man squirmed and
tried to get up. Summers gave his head a good-night lick with
the barrel of his rifle. The other man hadn't moved.

Men had begun to come from the Here's Howdy.

"Time to make tracks," Summers said.

Once free of the town, Higgins told him, "You was right, Dick, me wrong. I reckon you could say I was what they call purse-proud."

They walked up the hill, into the starlight and silence, into the good air, and then a voice reached them, singing. They halted and went on, and the voice came to them clearer. They halted again.

"Nocansee singin'," Higgins said.

> The warm of the sun,
> The wet of the rain,
> I sit and I hear
> That the prairie is wide.

"It's mostly his, but for the tune," Higgins said. "He sings better'n me."

"Shut up, Hig."

> The feel of the wind
> And the stir of the grass,
> These things I know
> And the prairie is wide.

The voice sounded clear and flowing as spring water, Summers thought, clear and flowing and sorrowful.

> The buffalo bawlin',
> The smell of meat cookin',
> I sit and I hear
> That the prairie is wide.

"Pity he don't sing more," Higgins said.

"Would you? Tell me that."

"Whoa up, Dick. What's rilin' you?"

Summers felt rage in him, and such a pity as would melt a man. "Would you in his fix? Makes a man want to goddamn God. He never had a chance, not one fuckin' chance."

31

GETS TIRESOME, just rustin' here," Higgins said. "I done smoked my throat raw."

"Hang to it," Summers told him.

"I'm hangin' all right, but not spooky. Who cares about them two measly bastards we banged on the head? Only about two nights' singin' in their pokes."

The sun had passed from straight overhead, burning as it lowered toward the hills. The women made out to be busy. Lije was coming back from watering the horses. Nocansee sat silent as if he never had sung a word.

Summers called out to Lije, "Keep the horses close in."

"I swear, Dick — " Higgins said and didn't say more.

"I keep tellin' you, you can't trust 'em, not the law in these diggin's. The butcher — Con, you know — he told me private and secret, not as he was too sure. But seems like the outlaws are the law. They don't want anyone hornin' in on their thievin's."

"Why not leave now?"

"As it is, they'd just foller."

"Strikes me you're seein' things under the bed."

"Maybe so."

Grasshoppers jumped and crawled along stems. A big one flew out in front of Lije's horses, making a buzz like a rattlesnake. High overhead two birds soared, looking down, Summers knew, with eyes that could make out a mouse. The women talked back and forth, now and then laughing. The sun lowered itself, inch by inch, and gave up some of its fire.

It was then that Summers saw the man. He pointed toward him, saying nothing.

On a prancing horse, to the jangle of spurs, the man rode to them. He had on a clean jacket and a clean shirt and a glinting star. His boots were new. "Got some business with you boys," he said. "I'm Stimson, deputy sheriff. I know your names."

Summers and Higgins got to their feet. Stimson stayed on his horse. He had a six-shoot Colt at his belt.

Higgins said, making out to be meek, "Pleased to meet you."

The women stood at the tepees, watching.

"That's nice," Stimson said. "Now it appears that you two beat up on a couple of our worthy citizens last night."

"Worthy?" Higgins asked. "Lord help us." Step by careful step he was working his way to one side of the horse, opposite Summers.

Stimson laughed a rich laugh. "Don't get me wrong. We don't make much of a scuffle. Boys will be boys."

"That's good to hear," Summers said.

"But robbery now, that's a different matter. I came for the pokes you took. Just hand them over, and there'll be no charges against you."

"You see any pokes, Dick?"

"Nary a one."

Stimson smiled, just biding his time. He had a full, confident face with whiskey burn in it. "We shall see what we shall see. Another little thing, men. The community has laws and licenses. There's a fee of twenty-five percent for wild animals brought in for sale. And an entertainer's license comes to twenty dollars a night. Sorry, gents, but you haven't paid."

Summers asked, "Who makes these laws?"

"They're mining camp laws. The sheriff enforces them with the help of his deputies."

"Who's the sheriff?"

"Henry Plummer, though that's not your concern."

"And him and you keep the money, that's if you tell him your takin's. We ain't of a mind to fork over."

Stimson touched the butt of his Colt. "I'm not here for trouble, but if you want it you'll get it. Hear me, dad?"

From the other side of the horse Higgins let his voice out in a screech. "Who you callin' dad? He's a better man than you'll ever be, you pus-gutted son of a bitch."

Stimson turned toward him. Summers grabbed Stimson by the arm, yanked him from the horse and thumped him on the ground. The pistol flew from the holster. Like a monkey Higgins ran in front of the plunging horse and gathered it up. Nocansee had got out of the way.

"Now," Higgins said mildly, "shall we go ahead with our talk?"

Stimson sat on his butt in the dust. "You'll pay for this. By God you'll pay. Wait till the sheriff hears."

Summers let a smile come to his face. "That's just what we'll do. Wait. You and us both." He called out to the women, "Break camp."

Lije came running up, his eyes wide. They took in what there was to see. "Don't need no help, I see." He sounded disappointed.

"We do, though," Summers said. "Bring the horses back, son. We're takin' off."

He turned to Higgins, who was holding the Colt steady on

Stimson. "Keep it lined up while I get his poke." Then, "Lord-amercy, it's right heavy."

"You dumb bastards." Stimson was still sitting in the dust.

"Now, Hig, I reckon that bob-tailed shootin' iron will fire, but it's shy on reach. I'll get my rifle. Happen he makes a run for it, I can shoot his lights out, fur as I can see him."

"You're making one goddamn big mistake," Stimson told them.

"Looks to me like you made the mistake," Summers answered. "Tryin' to rob two innocent citizens. Ain't there a law against that?"

"We'll forget the law. Keep the Colt, you jugheads. Give me my poke and my horse, and we'll call it even."

Higgins said, "Plumb reasonable, ain't he, Dick?"

"We'll let him go all right."

Lije had brought up the horses. The tepees were coming down. Nocansee held a nervous horse while Lije packed it.

"Hig, get a piece of rope, will you? We aim to see Mr. Stimson don't fall off his horse. Get some for his hands, too. He won't be usin' reins. First, though, fetch his horse. I'll keep him covered."

"They hang people for this," Stimson said.

"Sure do. Now get up and get on that horse, else I'll shoot you or club you with this here iron. That's the stuff. Now, Hig, tie his feet tight under the horse. Hands come next. We don't want no accidents and have to shoot the law."

The camp was clean. Horses packed. Horses saddled. Only the ashes of old fires left. Summers put a halter on Stimson's horse, saying, "I'll lead him, Hig." They were used to this way of travel. Horses for the two women, a horse for Nocansee with Lije leading on another, pack horses to be led by one rider or another, one travois that they might have to drop. Higgins swung into his saddle and called out, "Hi-yi."

Summers pointed almost due north, not knowing the way, knowing he would find it. They rode the stars pale and out and the sun up and the sun starting down, not stopping except to make water, and came to the time that Summers called a halt.

"No tepees tonight," he told the women. "Lije, looks like there's water down there a ways. Take the horses and see can you find some meat for the kettle. Hig and me's got work to do."

He untied the rope from Stimson's feet. Stimson groaned as he slid from the saddle. His legs folded under him when he tried to stand. From the ground he rubbed his knees with his tied hands. "You sons of bitches have crippled me."

"Watch he don't run away, Hig," Summers said. He walked to where the women were. He told them, "When I give the sign, come out with knives. Make like you wanted to butcher him some."

Nocansee said softly, "You wouldn't, though."

"Not one scratch, son."

When he returned, Stimson was on his feet. He held out his hands, and Summers freed them while Higgins held the Colt. "Now," Summers said, "take off your clothes, Mr. Deputy."

"Damned if I do!"

"Take 'em off or have 'em took off or knifed off, one way or t'other."

Slowly Stimson peeled off his jacket and laid it on the ground. Next came his shirt. "That suit you?"

"Get out of them pants. Boots, too."

"Come turn about, we'll nail you to the cross, Summers."

"Take 'em off, I said."

The man had a time with his new boots. He dropped his pants and stepped out of them and stood in his smallclothes.

Summers lifted his hand, and the women came screeching, knives in their hands. Stimson's eyes widened and stared. The blood left his face. He said, "Jesus Christ, no!"

The women ran a circle around him, squealing in Shoshone and Blackfoot while they swung the knives. Summers hushed them with a down stroke of his hand. They stood grinning and fingering the blades.

"Keep those squaws away," Stimson tried to shout, fear in his voice.

"Why?"

The answer came out in puffs. "You know why. They'll cut off my works — cock and balls."

Summers made out to consider. "What you think, Hig?"

"There wouldn't be any little Stimsons growin' up to be deputies. That's one thing."

"Act like white men for God's sake," Stimson asked.

"Why, I figured we were," Summers answered. "Just follerin' your lead."

"Take my poke. Welcome to it."

"We done took it."

"Take my horse."

"Got it a'ready."

"Just let me go."

Summers said to Higgins as if Stimson wasn't there, "You got a point. No more Deputy Stimsons. But look at it another way. Say we let the women have their fun. I got doubts he could make it back. Likely bleed hisself to death. I shy from murder."

The women went to screeching and dancing again, and again Summers stopped them.

"What's to do then?" Higgins asked.

"Seems a shame to say no to the womenfolk, but I don't know. Let's just turn him loose on the prairie."

Stimson croaked something.

"Way he is?" Higgins asked.

"Leave him his underclothes. He'll burn bad enough with them on."

"Boots?"

"I reckon. He'll have a heap of walkin' to do. Time he gets to the gulch, we'll be hell-and-gone, too far for his law to reach. Let's go."

They left him standing in his under-britches and shirt. He hadn't put on his boots yet.

As they reined away, Higgins said, "I could almost feel sorry weren't he such a bastard."

"Only right way I knowed to handle things," Summers said. "You got to keep solid in mind that a son of a bitch is a son of a bitch, no matter how come."

32

A NY WAY a man looked at it, age was a sorry thing. It came on a body gradual and then, almost all of a sudden, there it was. Take Dick Summers, Higgins thought as he led a horse to a tree to be tied up and shod. Not that Summers wasn't one hell of a man yet, but some of the spring had gone out of his step, and, in the mornings before he got loosened up, he walked gimpy, trying not to show it.

People who didn't know Summers would nod, accepting the signs. What would anyone expect in a man pushing seventy who had maybe pushed past it? Think to see him run and jump and holler and play hell with the ladies? Think to see him bracing one and all, wanting to fight? But to know the man was something else again, something different. It was to feel in himself the tired muscles, not springy now, and the ache in his joints, and want to sit down and bawl.

Higgins tied up the horse and went to get shoes, nails, hammer and trimmer. The horse was pretty frisky now that grass had sprung up and the signs of spring were at hand. It was shedding its rough winter coat. He would have brought it closer to camp, but the horse was a balky bastard and didn't like to be led. Better to tie it up here and walk for the tools than to yank the jughead along.

Summers and Lije had gone hunting. The women were sewing and working on skins. Nocansee hummed softly. It was a shame the boy didn't sing more, though he made a good partner in a duet when he could be coaxed to join.

These days Summers didn't have a great deal to say, though it wasn't age that hushed his tongue. Higgins knew that. It was the thought of Lije. It was trouble in his mind. The boy was a man now, full grown and past the time when most young bucks married. Not Lije. He had only smiled when told he should find him a wife, only smiled and shook his head as if, maybe, he couldn't decide whether he was red man or white and so couldn't settle which color he wished for a wife. But it wasn't that matter so much, Higgins knew, as what future there was for the boy. Where could he go, what could he do in a world where only old codgers could hope to drag along to the final end.

Higgins trailed back to the horse, carrying his tools. If the horse behaved decent, he'd be free in an hour, if only the shoes came close to fitting. What he needed was a forge. He went to work.

Old age now? He wasn't a young cock himself. Some of the snap had left him, and some of the things he used to do without breathing hard now made him suck air. Nothing to do about that, though. Just let the seasons roll — as if a man could stop them — and be satisfied with warmth and food and a good wife, and meat still to be had though hunting was harder. Be satisfied with what you had. Feel good that all debts were paid and some gold dust left over.

Today was no day to have the woes, anyhow. The sun, sliding west, was like a warm hand on his back. He felt the deep blue of the sky overhead. A breeze tickled the hair of the horse. When he looked east, he saw the greening rim of the valley and beyond it, he knew, was the endless reach of the plains. A man sitting pretty had to be happy.

He had just clinched the last horseshoe nail when he heard calls from the camp. He untied the horse, slapped its butt into freedom, picked up his gear and started walking.

Some way off, a man sat in the saddle yon side of the river while his horse and a pack animal drank. The words came faintly. "Bless you, brothers and sisters."

"By God," Higgins said to himself, "if it ain't Preacher Potter."

The women were talking, loud-voiced, against the voice of the stream. As he neared them, Higgins yelled, "Come across. Welcome, Brother Potter. Welcome."

Potter had put on weight, lost more of his side hair and gathered new wrinkles. Pulling up after he had forded the stream, he asked, "How doth His good people fare?"

"Jimdandy," Higgins answered. "I got a wife and a jug."

Potter, for a change, looked a little fazed. It was an instant before he answered, "I could make use of the latter."

"This is my wife, Little Wing. She's a Shoshone. This here is Brother Potter, Little Wing. He's a Methodist preacher."

"Bless you, Sister Higgins. Oh, hello, Nocansee. I didn't see you at first."

No need to tell him Nocansee didn't see, either. No need to tell him Nocansee caught on just the same.

Teal Eye told him, "My man and Lije, they be back soon. Gone hunting."

"I'll see them in time, the Lord willing."

"Git down. Git down."

Potter got off his horse with a grunt.

"Here," Higgins said, "I'll tie up your horses and see to 'em later. To a tired man a drink comes first. Hey, there's not enough on this pack horse to load a shotgun with."

"All my worldly goods."

Potter let himself down on the log he'd sat on so many years before. Higgins fetched the jug. "Good spirits," he said, "not that trade poison."

"Poison is the right word. It kills, but the Lord will wreak vengeance. Here's to you, Brother Higgins."

Potter took a nip and went on, "Total abstinence and over-indulgence are twin crimes. Heaven never meant us to do without something so good for soul and body or to drink it to excess."

"Second the motion."

"No meat till the men come," Little Wing said. She shook her head, worried. Food was the first and last thing for a guest.

"No hurry," Potter answered. "In fact I could well do without a few meals, though I doubt that I shall." He patted his stomach. "I confess to the small sin of near gluttony. May I have the jug again, Brother Higgins?"

"Wisht I carried more weight," Higgins said.

Hearing him, Little Wing sang out, "No sense. What you have be just right."

"Good woman," Higgins told Potter.

" 'A worthy woman, who can find? For her price is above rubies.' "

Summers' voice reached them from behind the tepees. "Game's scattered to hell and gone." He and Lije rode in, a single antelope on one of their two pack horses. "Well, if it ain't Brother Potter! A sight for sore eyes." He slid from his horse to shake hands.

"For these old eyes, too, though I doubt you'll find game in hell."

"You remember Lije."

"In another incarnation. In the person of a small boy. Bless you, Lije."

Lije said, "How-de-do," and shook hands.

"I have just met Sister Higgins," Potter said. "I have just

stated with biblical authority that a good woman is more precious than jewels."

Lije was unsaddling and unpacking the horses and would see them to grass. The women were busy with the antelope and the fire.

"He made a lucky pick all right," Summers said.

"Children?"

"Nary a one," Higgins answered. "The Lord ain't seen fit."

"He works in mysterious ways."

"Makin' and birthin' a baby is mysterious enough."

"He knows best. Trust in Him."

"Most ways I been blest all right. Just marryin' Little Wing for one thing."

"May I ask who married you?"

Higgins saw Summers squirm. Summers said, "As to that, it don't matter."

"It mattered to you," Potter told him.

"It was this way," Higgins said, seeing nothing but the truth to be told. "There wasn't no preacher around, but Summers remembered your words pretty good, and the Lord's Prayer came out fine."

"You mean Brother Summers presided?"

"Him and a Shoshone chief."

When Potter laughed, he laughed hearty.

Higgins was quick to say, "Knot couldn't be tied any tighter, not with dried rawhide."

"I believe you. But wouldn't you like a Christian marriage, under God's ordinance?"

"Me and Little Wing aim to see things through to the end."

"But a mere civil ceremony, so to speak?"

"It was civil enough for anybody."

"Still, Brother Higgins?"

Summers gave his white-toothed grin. "It don't hardly hurt at all."

"I'll put it to Little Wing." Higgins called her, and she came, her hands bloody from the antelope. "Brother Potter wants us to be married. Dick, too, seems like. It's up to you."

"I have you. You have me. We said so."

"Married a white man's way."

Little Wing looked at Potter, then at Higgins. "He is not a black robe."

"Not a black robe," Potter put in as if the idea didn't sit well with him, "but a true servant of God."

Teal Eye joined them, her hands bloody, too. "You say marriage? Then you get a white paper. It tells everyone."

"If Brother Higgins were to die before you, you would have no rights," Potter told her.

"He not die. I take care of him. And rights? What rights? What I care about rights?"

"Skip the rights," Summers said. "Point is, you want to get married again?"

"Little Wing?" Higgins asked.

Of a sudden she smiled. "Do again what is done. Why not? We eat big, and we sing."

Potter nodded his head, a smile touching his lips. "Sunup seems the chosen time. What about sunup tomorrow? Then I must leave you."

"So soon?" Summers asked. "What for?"

"In good time. In good time. After we've eaten. Might I have a taste from that jug again, Brother Higgins?"

"Excuse me all to — Excuse me, anyhow. Looks like marriage put it out of my mind."

A harsh spring wind came up as they were finishing their meal. Lije rose without speaking, and pretty soon Higgins saw smoke blowing up from the log cabin. It was warm enough when they entered with the fire cheery in the mud-and-stick fireplace. There were robes on the floor, and a wood block for Potter to sit on.

Potter rubbed his hands in front of the fire and made himself comfortable. "As I said I would tell you, I must be in Helena day after tomorrow."

Summers' voice was almost a growl. "Last Chance Gulch."

"Of course you have heard of it?"

"More'n I care to."

"There's a conference there. A meeting of the Methodist ministry. There's a growing support for my hope of a mission. I intend to promote it."

"Makes sense," Higgins said. "Whereabouts?"

"Undecided, but I have my eye on this region."

Summers lit his pipe and passed the twig to Higgins. The women sat cross-legged on the robes. The boys were sprawled out.

"Now for bigger news," Potter went on. "They are moving the Blackfoot agency from Fort Benton."

"What in hell for? Oh, pardon me, Brother Potter," Higgins said.

"It appears there is too much violence, too many drunken fights there."

"All the fault of the Indians, of course," Summers said with a lift to the corner of his mouth.

"Do you think for a moment I except the whites? They sell that foul whiskey and are prone to violence themselves."

"Sorry, Brother Potter."

"Where's the agency goin' to be at?" Higgins asked.

"That's the big point. As I am given to understand it will be right here in the Teton valley, only a few miles away."

Summers took his pipe from his mouth and forgot it. His eyes went from Potter to Higgins to Teal Eye, to Little Wing and the boys. At last he said, "Things are closin' in on us." He shook his head slowly.

"Yes, Brother?"

"An agency means a tradin' post, and a tradin' post grows into a town, and a hunter might as well lay down his rifle, for there'll be no game for fifty miles around. Hungry Indians trailin' in for rations and havin' to eat what the white men won't and stealin' to get money for rotgut. I can see it all. Lord Jesus, I can see it." He turned. "I wasn't cussin', Brother Potter." Now he remembered his pipe.

"Have faith. Have trust."

"It comes hard. It ain't possible."

Silence fell over them, silence and Summers' sadness, and the fire burned low, and the only voice was the voice of the breeze singing uneasy outside.

At last Summers raised his head. There were lines in his face Higgins hadn't seen before, or perhaps it was just the shadowed play of the fire which he had just put a stick on.

"I got a proposition, Brother Potter," Summers said. "I make it, but Lije and Teal Eye has to be willin'."

"Yes. Go on."

"I got a patch of land down in Missouri I could deed to you."

"What in the world for?"

"And some gold dust to boot."

Something inside him made Higgins say, "I'll put up my share," though he didn't know what the deal was. It was just that Summers looked so sad and so beat.

"I wait," Brother Potter said.

"My boy, Lije, he needs to know more, more about how to read and to write and to figger."

"And to love Jesus."

"If his stick floats that way."

Summers cleared his throat. He turned the dead pipe in his hand. "I was thinkin' maybe you could take him and teach him."

A little cry, quickly smothered, came from Teal Eye. Lije lifted his shoulders and sat straight, nothing showing in his face.

When Potter didn't answer, Summers went on, "He's comin' into a white man's world. He has to change himself to it. What good is what he knows now? It don't hatch any eggs that he can speak Blackfoot and Shoshone and English besides."

Brother Potter sat forward on his block. "This western world needs interpreters. You forget that."

"Maybe so. And maybe I'm plumb out of bounds, talkin' this way. So forget it."

"Brother Summers, I have listened. I have weighed your words. First let me say that I will take no money or land. If you feel like it, donate to the church. For the rest, I will take your boy and teach him as best I can and in all ways treat him as if he were my own."

A wail came from Teal Eye. She cried out, "No. No."

"Think of our son, little duck. Think only of him."

Into her crying she got out, "I know. I know."

Potter turned to meet Lije's eyes. "What do you say, my son?"

The boy's voice sounded lifeless. "I do what my father says."

"Amen."

33

To Teal Eye the morning sun looked angry. It rose, bit by bit, and glared at the party, at Brother Potter with his book and Higgins and Little Wing standing side by side while he said the words. Summers and Lije were at one side, and Nocansee held her hand.

But no, she thought, squinting again against the morning light. The sun wasn't angry. It wasn't anything. It just watched, and a person could see anger or sorrow in it if so he wished. Or he could see nothing at all except for the blazing ball.

"'Our Father who art in heaven...'"

How many suns had looked down on them, at Lije, the baby, at Lije, the young boy, at Lije as he stood now, his face unshowing. How many winds had pushed him and pulled? How many moons had lighted his steps? They were all one, all one with the now that was then. She mustn't cry, not during prayer.

" 'Thy kingdom come . . .' "

Nocansee pressed her hand.

" 'Thy will be done . . .' "

It was over, too soon over, and Higgins kissed Little Wing while Brother Potter smiled.

"Now we must be off," Brother Potter said when the hand-shaking and good-wishing were done. "Are you about ready, Lije?"

"I got the horses saddled and tied up over there just a ways," Summers said. "I'll get 'em."

They were silent while he was gone, silent before the hurt of the parting soon to be. Even Brother Potter had no words.

Summers came back, leading four horses.

Teal Eye dared to speak, hearing her voice come out frail. "You have everything, Lije? You sure?"

"Everything, Mamma." He turned his eyes from her face.

Brother Potter shook all hands again. "We'll see you soon. Don't worry about Lije. Have faith."

Summers helped him into the saddle. Lije shook hands with Little Wing and Higgins. He came to his father, and they shook, man to man, smiling with smiles that weren't smiles. Nocansee threw his arms around Lije, saying, "Brother. Little brother." It was all right for blind men to cry.

She held Lije tight, not screaming her inside screams. All she could say was, "Be safe, my son."

Lije mounted his horse. Summers came to her and took her hand. She felt tension in his. Brother Potter led away, and she watched and watched, Summers beside her, until they rode out of sight. Then she turned and went into the tepee.

She lay down on their bed and let quiet grief take her, hearing movement and voices outside that had no meaning.

Her man was right. Lije had to go. But why was the god of Brother Potter so cruel? Why should a baby, torn from her body, be torn away at his manhood? Would she see Lije again?

Ever? Who, what could fill the space he had left? When again could her heart be full?

Nocansee came in and sat down beside her, saying nothing, only taking her hand, and the keening she had held in broke from her throat. It was keening for death.

But Lije wasn't dead, she told herself fiercely. He had just gone away. She choked off her cries.

She didn't know when Nocansee left, he was so light-footed. Little Wing took his place, telling her she should eat. Eat when she had no stomach, no insides but the hurting heart? Summers came in, once, then again and again, and his hand stroked her head, and he kept on saying, "It will be all right, little duck. Don't take on so hard."

Noon came, and afternoon, and she didn't care. When she napped, it was only to wake up with the pain and the emptiness in her. Something told her that never again would she see her son.

It was dark when she wakened as Summers lay down beside her. He hugged her close. Two people but only one, she thought, two people made one by their sorrow.

Grief, she thought. Grief and the body, and body needing body in grief.

She helped her man enter her.

34

IT'S BEEN one bitch of a winter, but now I think maybe its
backbone is broke," Higgins said.

He was talking just to be talking, talking loud against
the wind that was trying to outholler him.

On days like this one, Summers thought, there was nothing
to do but sit in the cabin, smoke and once in a while throw a
log on the fire, nothing to do but listen to the wind that tore
around the corners and went shouting away as another blast
came. A man could hardly stand up outside. Beside him was a
ragged deck of cards that he and Higgins had played Old
Sledge with until they tired of the game.

It had been a bitch of a winter all right, snow and blizzard
and the quiet cold that crept through the clothes, the skin and
the muscles, driving for the last flutter of life.

"Anyhow, this here's a chinook, a damn hard chinook but a

chinook just the same." Like Higgins, he was talking for talk's sake.

Teal Eye was doing beadwork by the little light a window let in, its panes shaken and veiled by the blowing snow. Nocansee was working with a deer skin to make it useful and soft. Little Wing was chopping meat on a block. A mouse peeked down from the sod roof.

The deer had plowed down from the mountains and often an elk, and their meat was stringy and tough and their bellies full of chewed wood. No trouble in shooting them. They stood alone, ganted up, or yarded together in the brush, maybe thinking a bullet was better than torment, and their hides hung to their bones with no fat between. Buffalo? They were long gone, to the south or wherever, moving slow under the weight of their hair. Blue meat, it would be, when a man butchered one.

The cabin was warm enough but not stuffy, as it would have been if he and Higgins had built it tight. Loose-built, it let in the whiff of horse manure now and then. In bad weather horses always crowded around a cabin or barn or tumble-down building. Given time, they would butt and shoulder it down. Damn nuisance, but it saved trying to catch them up in the open. The mouse sat still and beady-eyed, soaking up heat.

The cabin shook to a harder blast, and Higgins said through his pipe smoke, "I never knowed it to blow so hard without snow or rain comin' after. This time I'm bettin' on rain."

Summers rose. His bad leg almost let him down, the damn thing. "Foot's asleep," he said. He made it to the door and opened it a few inches and looked out, looked out at nothing but sweeping snow and the nose in front of his face.

He closed the door, sat down again and said, "Ground blizzard. It will sweep the flats clean."

"And leave hellish drifts."

"March and April are notionable months."

"Bad as people," Higgins said. They relighted their pipes. "Speakin' of notions —" Higgins began and fell silent.

Summers didn't speak, knowing that Higgins would go on in time.

Teal Eye stirred. "I hope Lije not out in this wind." She kept thinking about Lije.

"Brother Potter look after him," Little Wing said as she scooped the cut meat in a pot.

Nocansee lifted his head, perhaps having heard the little movement of the mouse. The mouse watched.

Higgins said again, "Speakin' of notions, I kind of got one in my bonnet."

"Let it out."

"Or me'n Little Wing have."

"So?"

"She hankers to see her folks."

Summers puffed on his pipe and found slow words to say, "Can't blame her none."

"Not to leave us," Teal Eye cried out.

"Just for a spell," Higgins told her. "Long enough to get there, visit a while and come back."

He meant it, Summers knew. He meant it, but who could tell? Not even God himself.

"It is for good," Teal Eye said to her beadwork. A gust shook the cabin, carrying her words to wherever it went.

Little Wing brought the pot over and nested it in the fire.

Higgins said, "She's got a right to see her kin. Been a long time. I figure we would take off when the first flowers bloom so's to be back, Teal Eye, before frost sets in."

Little Wing was making happy noises in her throat. Nocansee kept working the stiff from the hide. The mouse ducked back in its hole, stirring up a trickle of dust.

Things were closing in and closing out, Summers thought. Life narrowed as the years grew. It crowded and narrowed. With Higgins and Little Wing gone?

He puffed, but his pipe had gone out.

◤ ◥ ◢

They were ready to go, horses saddled and packed, one tepee down, the cabin and grounds looked over again for items maybe forgotten.

"You should have picked better horses, 'stead of these old pelters," Summers said. It was like Higgins to take the four oldest of the nine horses they had.

"They'll get us there, don't you worry," Higgins answered.

They were all standing around, waiting, holding the parting off for this minute. Little Wing and Higgins just fiddled with the reins in their hands, not up to goodbyes quite yet.

The day was good, at least. The spring sun was warm, lighting a sky without a wisp of cloud in it. The trees were about to leaf out, their buds swollen and sticky, soon to give birth. It was a time of birds and bird songs.

Little Wing said, "We come back. Look for us. Look before snow."

Sure, Summers thought, they'd come back maybe. Maybe on some fair afternoon they'd return to pick up the life they were leaving. Maybe.

The two women hugged each other, both crying. Little Wing laid a hand on Nocansee's shoulder and said, "I hope good things." She hugged Summers. Higgins helped her on to her horse and turned. "You good old son of a bitch," he said and swung around fast. "Goodbye, goddamnit."

"Keep your scalp, old pardner."

As they rode off, turning once to wave, Teal Eye came to Summers and put her head in the hollow of his shoulder, more for his sake, he thought, than her own. He kept control of his voice. "Hardest lesson of all is to learn to say goodbye."

Inside their tepee lay Higgins' cased fiddle. "Hell's sake," Summers said. "He forgot. I'll have to catch up with him." A scrap of tanned deerskin lay on the fiddle. It had words on it, written in charcoal.

"Nocansee you can lern to play it good."

35

DUST ROSE upstream across the river. It rose and hung there, wavering just a little to the breath of air. Men would be working there, working with big shovels drawn by horses, tearing up the buffalo grass.

Summers had ridden once close enough to see. Loaded wagons waited and running gears piled high with logs and raw lumber, and the sounds of men reached him and the knock of axes and the scrape-scrape of saws. Some soldiers moved around, doing nothing but watch. There was to be the new agency. It was located about four miles away from his camp, between the Teton and a small creek that flowed at the far side of the valley and joined the Teton a short piece lower down.

He sat his horse and watched the dust rising. Soon enough

the agency officers would arrive and probably more soldiers and then a straggle of Indians coming to see if the white man lived up to his promises. He wouldn't.

Put down another marker to judge time by. Let it stand in the story. Big doings. A new agency, and it would give way to time, too, though nobody thought so, not with change just taking place.

Everything was new as of its time. And everything was old, or would be with the years. Nothing stayed put. Men came with their big ideas, looking to a future that would laugh at their work. Why not let things be? Why the hurry to play hell with what was? That was the way of man. That was the way of men who bred and increased and reached out.

He fingered his cold pipe and put one hand to his knee, which didn't bother him so much in warm weather. Pretty soon he'd make sure his loose horses hadn't strayed.

In these long sunset and twilighted days the workingmen would knock off long before dark, and they and off-duty soldiers would be banging away with shotguns and rifles, and the game would run and be lost or lie crippled and dying with the men too eager for fresh targets to follow the blood trails. Sport, they would call it.

No one could fault a man who shot meat for the kettle or frying pan, but damn the man who shot to be shooting and killed to be killing. While in camp they had been hearing shots, some too close, where before there had been silence.

Lately he and the family had had to make do with grouse and mallards and cottontails and the trout of the Teton. Once in a while a deer. Once in a long while an elk. Never a buffalo now. Not here. Not hereabouts.

From here he could see the tepee and the cabin. Taking No-cansee with her, Teal Eye had gone down the river to see if the June berries were ripe. She kept busy. She always had, but now it was as if she moved so's not to think. She didn't complain, but some of the sparkle had left her, some of the spirit.

Her eyes sometimes looked empty. He could understand. Lije gone, and no word from him. Higgins and Little Wing far away with the Shoshones. For company just himself and Nocansee, and mostly it was only old talk they could talk, talk they'd talked before. Often they were silent, the only sound the sad sound of the fiddle that Nocansee practiced on.

He watched the dust rising and thought that for two bits he'd leave the Teton if he knew where to go.

The dust rose and, closer, another weaker trail of it that seemed to lead toward his camp. He made sure his Hawken was loaded and rode down to meet it.

Three Indians dragged up on their poor-flesh cayuses. It was a time before he recognized Heavy Runner. He left the saddle and made the peace sign and motioned for them to come forward.

Heavy Runner got off his horse and said in Blackfoot, "We come in peace and to talk, Bear Maker." He looked tired and drawn, and his buckskins weren't proud. "I bring two good men."

"Come, friends, and smoke. My lodge is yours."

The other two Indians dismounted, and Heavy Runner named names that Summers didn't catch. One of them tied up the horses.

The tepee was the proper place for sober palaver, and Summers led the way to it and invited them to sit down. He lighted his pipe, pointed it in the four directions and passed it around.

They sat and talked, as Indians did, avoiding and circling around the point that was to be made. Summers told them, "My woman has gone to pick berries. The pot is empty. But whiskey I have."

Heavy Runner shook his head. "It kills my people."

"It is not trade whiskey, not poison."

Heavy Runner took a long look at him. Summers rose and got the jug. They were old men. They swallowed small.

At last Summers said, "You can tell me. My ear is open."

"My people die," Heavy Runner said as if measuring his words. "My young men go crazy. It is the firewater."

"From whiskey traders?"

Heavy Runner bowed, head and body, and his hand moved, saying yes. "They travel the whiskey road, the traders, from Fort Benton to Fort McLeod across the Medicine Line, and they sell as they go. Sell to my people."

"In the wind I have heard."

"So many die. So many young braves drink it, steal for it, steal horses, anything, for to trade."

"I believe you."

"The white soldiers, the white chiefs, hear of stealing. They hear of white men rubbed out. They do not like it. They hate us. But what to do with my young braves? A chief he is not a general. He can speak but not order, and his words fly away."

Heavy Runner's friends hadn't spoken. They sat listening, their hands folded unless used in the yes sign.

"Why, friend, come to me?" Summers asked.

"My village is friendly village. We do not want the trouble. It is Mountain Chief whose men kill. They come across the Medicine Line and steal and sometime kill, but to the white men all Indians are Indians."

"It is so. My heart is low because the white man is foolish."

Summers waited and then put the question again. "But why come? What can I do?"

Heavy Runner's tired face lifted, and his eyes met Summers' square on. "Because we need you."

"For what, my friend?"

"In our camp we need a white man, a good man, a wise old man to tell us."

"I wouldn't know wise words to say."

"A good white man in our camp shows everybody we are good people."

"Don't bet on it. But is it protection my friend thinks about?"

"Someone to guide us the right way. Someone to explain to the white chiefs before trouble comes. That is you, Bear Maker, for we are poor in words."

"I must talk in my mind, Heavy Runner. I think no but maybe yes. If it is no, we are still friends."

"My lodge is always yours."

"Where is it?"

"On what is called the Marias. It is sometimes good hunting. It is big land, far as the eye sees, and our people, the Blackfeet, they be not so many."

"I will think."

The Indians rose, shook hands, walked out to their horses and rode away.

After they were gone, Summers climbed into the saddle again. The sun was halfway past its high, and he hadn't yet seen to the loose horses or shot anything for the pot. There was time for both, if he didn't have to look too long for game. That was the question, what with workers from the agency banging around.

Sometimes two or three of them rode by his camp, not stopping, their eyes curious as if they saw the last of a race, as if he were out of place in the world, something left over from the first days. He reckoned they weren't so far off at that.

A shot sounded from behind a thicket. He put his horse to a lope and rounded the edge of it. A man stood there, a rifle dangling from his hand, and a horse lay thrashing in the grass. "Hold it!" Summers shouted.

The man turned, his eyes wide. "I didn't mean . . ." The horse had climbed to its feet. It stood still with the dull look of slow suffering.

"Goddamnit, kill it!" Summers told the man. "You gut-shot it, now kill it."

The rifle still hung from the man's hand. "I couldn't — I mean I can't — not a horse."

Summers lurched from the saddle. He took aim with the

Hawken, dropped it, grabbed the man's repeating rifle from his loose hand and shot the horse in the forehead just above the eyes. The horse went down, quivering, and lay still.

"You can still brag it was your gun that kilt him," he said. He swung the man's rifle against a rock, then swung it again. "You dumb son of a bitch. Best horse I own."

"But I tell you, I didn't mean . . ."

He wasn't a man but a boy, a boy with fear and regret in his eyes. "It looked like an elk or maybe a deer, so . . ."

"So you just fired away, like a fool. Shoot at anything that moves, just to be killin'."

"It was a new rifle, a Henry repeater. I wanted to see . . ."

"To see if you could get yourself a prime horse. I ought to give you a runnin' start and see do you like lead in your ass."

"I can pay you, in time, I mean. And I'm sorry, sir. I acted the fool." The boy did look sorry, sorry and pained, a boy at a loss.

Summers sat slow in the grass. It wasn't the bad leg that let him down, not it alone. It was the weight on his shoulders, the heaviness in his head and the let-down feeling that followed rage.

"Christ," he said, "there are too many of you. Pick up your rifle and go."

"I don't know that I understand."

"I said you are too many. Just go, boy."

He sat with the dead horse and the live one and watched the boy walk away. Likely the rifle wasn't damaged too much.

On the ride home, for lack of better meat, he shot the heads off two jackass rabbits. They would be tough as bull hide but better than nothing.

As he dressed them out, the thought was with him that the time had come to go. He would have to talk to Teal Eye, but the sooner the better would suit him. To gut-shoot a poor, god-damn horse!

By first light they had the tepee down and the horses packed. Teal Eye looked at the bare earth where the tepee had stood. The unknowing grass would cover it, cover where she and Summers had loved, where Lije had been born, where the days, the happy days were, and it would be as if they never had lived, never talked or laughed or had friends or sat by the shores of the Teton. The air was empty and torn where the tepee had risen.

But Summers was right. It was time to go, and she had said a sad yes to him, and Nocansee, like Lije before him, had said, "I do what my father says."

They were mounted and ready to leave when Summers got off his horse. Teal Eye watched him gather twigs and branches and old bark and carry them inside the cabin. Coming out, he laid a little trail of gunpowder from cabin to ground. He struck a spark with flint and steel.

The cabin was burning bright before they had gone far.

Looking back, Teal Eye said, "No one would know, not ever."

Summers nodded his head. "Best to leave it as we found it. That's what I'm thinkin'. New-like but old."

36

It was cold in the village of Heavy Runner, cold everywhere in the country of the Marias, so cold that the lungs hurt with breathing and face and fingers turned white with frost if a man didn't take care. When, inside the tepee at last, he put his feet toward the fire, they caught fire with itch. People stayed close and tight in their lodges, their bodies covered with blankets or robes in spite of the fires they kept burning.

There was sickness in camp, too, smallpox, the gift of the white man to the red. The village wasn't big — maybe twenty lodges on one side of the river, eleven on the other. Its size didn't keep it from being hungry.

Summers slapped his arms across his chest and made and unmade fists with his hands. He had been lucky enough to get a deer in his sights. He would divide it as far as it went if he could get it to camp. His nostrils were narrowed with frost. Each pant of his breath made a cloud.

Even so, he thought as he ordered his hands to make use of the knife, his lodge fared better than most. He put out set lines in the Marias, chopping holes in the ice when he had to, and caught mostly catfish but often a pike or a trout. They were good food, though they didn't stay with a man like buffalo meat. The Indians wouldn't eat fish, calling them the underwater people, but Teal Eye had outgrown such notions.

He looked up from the work of gutting the deer and slapped himself again. The blood and the entrails had warmed his hands, but soon enough the blood would turn sticky and freeze if he left it on. The day was clear, the ground mostly windswept and bare, but the sun was cold brass and the breeze had icicle fingers.

It had been different when first he came to the Marias. High summer then, and the sun shone warm on a world without limits, broken by the spires of the Sweetgrass Hills and the shadows of western mountains. There were buffalo about, not too many but enough for the Indians, and he had come upon hunting parties on their buffalo horses, riding wild in the herds, shooting arrows or old Hudson's Bay muskets when they came within range. The squaws pounded the meat, mixing the flesh with wild berries and grease, making pemmican for winter use.

He wiped his hands dry on the hair of the deer, slid the knife in its case and put on his cold mitts.

Once he had made a two-day journey eastward and south and turned back when he came upon hide-hunters and heard the boom of their guns. A good killing rifle, one man had told him, a Sharps, and a bullet most anywhere would knock a bull down.

He led the pack horse close to the deer. It was a good piece to camp, and some of the way was broken country. That was how it was along the Marias, broken country, but once a man was out of its gorges and channels the land swept away. Good buffalo country come summer. Deer in the swales.

He took off his mitts, lifted the deer carcass to the horse and lashed it on. The horse stood, patient and cold, and the breeze played along its winter hair. The saddle horse was cold, too. Its eyes seemed to say he was at fault for the weather. "Not my doin's," he told it through stiff lips. He got himself into the saddle. In times like this his leg acted up. Teal Eye would put hot blankets on it.

The village was silent, deserted, it seemed like, except for a few skinny and shivering dogs, except for the smoke rising from tepees. A dog could stand a heap of cold. So, far as that went, could an Indian. So could an old mountain man.

He pulled up in front of his lodge, and Teal Eye came out. "Go back in," he told her. "Too damn cold."

"You cold, too," she said. "You colder."

He carried the carcass inside the tepee. "Back in a shake," he said. His smile felt numb. "Don't let the fire go out."

He led the horses away, freed one, and put the other on picket, close at hand. When the snow was deep, he would feed it chopped-up cottonwood bark. They would keep it alive, barely.

The warmth of the tepee seeped into him. He took off his heavy capote, his old coonskin cap and clumsy mitts. "From here I can feel the cold of you," Nocansee told him. Nocansee had a fine face and a gentle smile. A body learned to forget his eyes. "I am making up a song," he went on. "I am calling it 'Coyotes on a Snowy Night.'"

"Sounds good, son."

Nocansee plucked at a string on his fiddle. He could play it real good already, almost as good as Higgins. On warmer days Indians asked him to play. They were kind to him. Indians always were kinder than white men to people with miseries.

"I am hunting for words, my father. What do coyotes cry for?"

"For full bellies, I reckon."

"Those are not good words for song."

"For mates, then." Summers was sorry he had spoken. Blind

men didn't find mates. He added quickly, "Or just for the joy of singin', for bein' alive."

"It could be. Sometime I think lonesomeness."

"They ain't too often alone."

"Maybe they sing for the sun, for the light."

Yeah, for the light! For the light. For eyes to see with. But maybe Nocansee didn't make the connection. He wasn't sorry for himself, not by any signs.

Summers said, "I'm thinkin' you're wrong. They got keen ears and fine noses, and you never hear 'em singin' to the sun."

Summers stepped over to help Teal Eye with the deer. "We will give it to the sick," she said.

"Savin' just a bit for ourselves."

He felt gentleness for her. That was Teal Eye, to give to the sick, to visit lodges where sickness was, unafraid for herself. It was lice she couldn't stand. It seemed like she was forever examining seams, combing hair and boiling clothes in the old boiler he had picked up once at Fort Benton.

"It went away from my head," she said. "Heavy Runner, he came. He wants to talk."

"What about?"

She shrugged.

"I feel trouble," Nocansee said, raising his head. "Bad trouble."

"No trouble, son," Summers answered, but there was a shade of doubt in his mind. Sometimes Nocansee, without eyes, saw farther than others. "We will eat first. No hurry."

"No," Teal Eye said. "First we warm your leg. It hurts. I can tell."

"Later, little duck. Later."

Heavy Runner and his two wives were inside his lodge when Summers showed up. After greetings, one of them said, "We go visit your woman. It is all right?"

"She will be happy."

He and Heavy Runner sat by the fire and smoked, not speaking until Heavy Runner said, "I think sometimes to take a new squaw, a young one for the hard work. My women grow old."

Summers puffed smoke.

"I do not know," Heavy Runner went on. "Two sons I have, good boys, good hunters one time, and much meat was in camp. They are gone."

"It is the way of the young."

"Gone for firewater, so I am thinking. Gone to the camp of the traders. They not here anymore. They go always."

"It is too cold."

Heavy Runner spit into the fire. "Cold. What is cold? Never cold with hot fire in the guts."

"They will come back. They are not wild."

"Wild with drink in them, wild for more of it, so they will steal and make mad the white chiefs. That I think I see."

Summers hitched nearer the fire, easing his leg. By and by Heavy Runner would come to what was first in his mind.

At last he spoke. "My friend, it is said a man by name Malcolm Clarke has been killed."

"It is in the wind. Him that worked at Fort Benton. By Blackfoot name White Lodge Pole or Four Bears. This much I know."

"It was not my people and not my sons who made him dead. It was young men from Mountain Chief's band."

"You know them, my friend? You know who?"

"If I know, I do not say."

"Not your business, you say then?"

Heavy Runner added wood to the fire. A louse crawled at the end of a hair, and he saw it with sideways eyes, picked it off, cracked it with his teeth and spit it out.

"They came today. Two. Word-bringers. What you call — "

"Messengers?"

"Messengers from the white chiefs."

"To say it is your business?"

"All Blackfoot chiefs called to meet at the new agency."

"Who were the messengers?"

"Two men, I have said. They know Indian talk. They carry papers."

"You know the men?"

"Maybe so, maybe not. It does not matter."

"My mouth is tired with questions. Tell what you want to tell."

"Messengers do not say what for to meet, only to be at the new agency on the Teton. They tell me so and go quick to tell other chiefs."

"You have not said the time."

"Soon. What you call the first day of the new year."

"Jesus Christ, that's soon enough. Meet in the dead of winter!"

"So it was said. Cold trip, my friend."

"And not short. Three sleeps, I figure."

"That many. Maybe little more. Maybe not."

Heavy Runner sighed and looked up. His voice sounded humble. "So now I am needing you. So now we are needing you."

Summers waited.

"Now you will speak for us. Yes, my friend?"

Summers stretched out one leg and tried to rub the ache from his knee. Three sleeps in the cold and a bum leg to boot, all for a parley that wouldn't get anywhere.

"I do not know for what good," Summers said, "but yes, I will speak."

37

BREATHING and snorting white, they and their horses paused at the rim of the Teton valley. They had reached it from the north and east, and on this clear and biting morning Summers could tell just about where his old camp was. Beyond it the great range of the mountains reared sharp and white against the blue of the sky. Closer, a mile or so downhill, lay the few buildings of the new agency. They looked rough and raw, as if they had not come to peace with the land, if ever they could. A flag flew there. And farther, downstream, he saw a building or two, the beginnings maybe of a new town.

At his side Heavy Runner pointed to the boldest of the mountains, the one Summers felt almost kin to, and spoke in Blackfoot. "It was there, on top, that I learned and I saw. There, long ago. I was almost a man, and I looked for my medicine. I climbed to the top. I went without water or food, and I waited and waited, and my strength left me, and I fell to the ground. Then came the great white bear and helped me down."

Heavy Runner patted his side where, under his wraps, Summers knew, his medicine pouch hung. A man didn't ask what was in one.

The trees stood bare, winter-dead, in the valley. It would take the big medicine of spring to lift them and drape them with life. The ground was dead and bare, too, except for a here-and-there snowdrift. No game moved. No tracks showed. The only animals were some horses hitched close to the agency. And here, once, was the purest valley of all.

They rode down to the agency, four chiefs with two head men each and Summers himself. Troopers waited for them, troopers so bundled up that only the light blue stripes on their breeches showed what they were. All of them carried carbines.

"Tie your horses up here," one of them said and pointed to a hitch rack. "Leave any weapons at the door."

Summers translated for the chiefs. When he handed in his old Hawken, the soldier looked at it and said, "By God, if that ain't a relic. Shoot true?"

"I been known to hit a few things."

"What you doin' with these redskins?"

"Me heap medicine man."

The trooper looked at him. "All right, I guess."

The weapons weren't much — a couple of muskets, one spear, and bows and arrows tipped with metal. A poor lot, but right for a peace party.

At another season the chiefs, at least, would have worn feathered headdresses. Now they had blankets and pieces of fur as coverings. They looked at one another before entering the building, perhaps wishing they'd brought their war bonnets along, hard to pack right though they were.

They were led into a large room with a desk and chairs in it.

A cast-iron fireplace tried to fight off the cold. Two men sat behind the desk, and right behind them stood Lije.

"By God, Lije!" Summers said, ignoring the two men.

Lije stood stiff as if trained to it until one of the men said, "At ease."

They shook hands. Lije hurried to ask, "My mother, my brother, how are they, my father?"

"All fine. Fine and dandy."

One of the men had swung around. "Father?"

"Most people have one, livin' or dead," Summers answered. "This here's my son."

The man swung back. The Indians were seating themselves on the floor against the walls. Summers joined them. A soldier was clearing the chairs away. Scattered in the room were half a dozen others. Though told to be at ease, they stood pretty stiff.

One of the men behind the desk came to his feet. "The meeting will come to order," he said. "I am General Sully, superintendent of Indian affairs for the territory of Montana, and at my side is United States Marshal William F. Wheeler."

Lije was translating what he said.

"As I call out names will you please indicate your presence? Our interpreter is Many Tongues, who knows English, Blackfoot, Shoshone and, I understand, some Salish."

Sully was in a blue uniform with brass buttons and gold braid on it and other trappings that meant something or other. Wheeler had a star on his chest.

"Now. Heavy Runner?"

Heavy Runner raised his hand.

"Little Wolf?"

Little Wolf signaled here.

"Mountain Chief?"

The chiefs were silent, their eyes fixed straight ahead.

"Where is Mountain Chief?"

No answer.

"Sir," Lije said, "they do not know."

"They haven't said anything."

"Because they do not know, sir."

Sully said to Wheeler, "The man we wanted most. Humph."

"He and his killers."

Sully turned back. "All right. Big Leg?"

Big Leg was on hand.

"You are all Piegans. Right?" He pointed. "Then you. Gray Eyes, is it?"

The man answered in Blackfoot, and Lije translated, "Gray Eyes of the Bloods."

"My red brothers," Sully said, "we come to talk to you. We come in peace, we come hoping peace, but, peace or not, it is yours to say."

Lije was keeping up with him.

"Last year, the year just closed, white men have lost one hundred horses a month to Indian thieves. Fifty-six white men have been killed. The latest was one you all know. Malcolm Clarke. We tell you now, in friendship: no more stealing, no more killing."

Wheeler interrupted to say, "And that's not all."

The chiefs and their head men sat silent and motionless, only their eyes moving, to the speaker, to the standing soldiers, to one who put wood on the fire.

"We know who killed Clarke," Sully went on. "Mountain Chief's men, by name Pete Owl Child, Eagle Rib, Bear Chief, Black Weasel and Black Bear. They must be turned over to us. Do you understand?"

Now Heavy Runner said in his halting English, "My friend. Indian name Bear Maker. He talk? Yes?"

"We didn't come to hear arguments," Wheeler said.

"Where's the harm? All right, Bear Maker."

Summers got to his feet and walked, trying not to limp, to face the two men. He must watch his words, speak as good English as he could. He had had a mighty short time to review what he knew, to sum up time and change, to talk to old men who knew some things he didn't, to be sure of right.

"For the record, your name?" Sully said. For the first time Summers noticed a man in the corner was taking notes.

"Dick Summers." It took some doing but he added, "sir."

"Richard Summers?"

"If you want it that way?"

Sully smiled. "You are something of a legend, Mr. Summers."

"Comes from living so long."

"You have spent all your years in the west?"

"Most of 'em." Again he added, "sir."

"Would you care to tell us how old you are?"

Now Summers let himself smile. "As they say, too old to suck, too tough to die. Make it seventy-odd. I'm not too sure."

"All the time with the red men?"

"No, sir. Sometimes. Sometimes friend, sometimes not."

"I know all this, Dick," the general said, letting his manner loosen. "The record doesn't."

"It's all right."

"So now we'll be glad to hear what you have to say."

Summers took a breath. "It's all so one-sided."

"One-sided?"

"You know how many horses have been stolen, how many white men have been killed and who killed Malcolm Clarke. I don't deny any of that. Neither do the chiefs."

Lije was keeping right up with him.

"But you don't know how many red men have been killed. I doubt you know who killed Mountain Chief's brother right in Fort Benton."

"We think we're about to find the answer on the last point," Wheeler put in.

"It's like as if red lives don't count," Summers continued.

Sully nodded his head, not as if he much wanted to.

"You want Clarke's killers turned over to you, and, I would guess, all the stolen stock returned."

"That's right."

"That's right, sir, but it's wrong. It can't be done. Think on it, General. Like you know, there's three divisions to the Black-foot nation — Piegan, Blood and Blackfoot proper. Each division is divided into villages or bands under chiefs like you see here. You ask one division or one band to take men or horses from another, and you got civil war."

"I doubt it will be that bad."

"It won't be because they won't and can't do it."

"I honor your feelings, Dick, but we act under orders."

"Whose orders?"

"Orders come from ranking officers under the direction of Washington."

There was an edge in Sully's tones now, and Summers knew he had overstepped. "General, sir, would you listen to me just a little while longer?"

The edge wore off fast. "Sure, Dick."

"The government set aside lands for the Blackfeet. I got it in mind that was the treaty of eighteen fifty-five. The land stretched from the mountains, the continental divide, clean to the Missouri and from the Canadian line to the Teton or Sun River, I ain't sure which."

"Go on."

"If the land belongs to the Blackfeet, wouldn't you think they would own what's underground, too, like the gold they're minin' at Last Chance Gulch? Wouldn't you think the grass belonged to the Indians and the soil and the things that grow on both, like the buffalo the hide-hunters are killing off?"

"Dick, those are such vexed questions, questions of policy, of politics, of ownership, of human rights, red and white. I'm a military man. I can't answer you."

"No, sir. Neither can I, but I can sure understand how the Indian feels. Wouldn't you, in his fix?"

"Probably." Sully's smile seemed small and sad. "Let's grant all you say is true. It is true, too, that stock is stolen and men killed. Do you have a way out of that?"

"I do, sir."

Wheeler said, "Oh, for Christ's sake!"

"We might as well hear it."

"Put an end to the whiskey trade, that's what. I'm not speaking of honest whiskey. I'm speaking of the poison the traders sell, all the way from Fort Benton to Fort McLeod. That's what drives young Indians crazy. That's what makes them steal and kill. And that's what's killing off twenty-five per cent of the Blackfeet, men and some women, every year. Close that goddamn trail, General. Close it and see."

Sully said "Hmm" through closed lips.

"I reckon you never tasted it, and for sure you better not. It's straight alcohol watered down some, colored and flavored with black molasses and plugs of tobacco and fired up with red pepper and capsicum. Jesus, that stuff, one teaspoon, would rot out a wash boiler. Close the trail. Arrest the traders. Thank you, General Sully. Thank you, Wheeler."

General Sully sighed and rose. "I have listened and thank you. There is much to be said for your position, much right in your words, but I do not make policy. I execute it."

He looked around at the chiefs. "The men who murdered Malcolm Clarke must be surrendered to us. The stolen stock must be returned. All that within the next two weeks. If it is not done, we have no recourse but to declare a state of war with the Blackfoot nation."

As they filed out, Summers halted and said to Lije, "Don't be discouraged, son. You're on the right path."

"I am sad."

"You'll get over it, boy, and we might have done some good today."

Once in a while a man had to lie.

38

L IJE SUMMERS stood back of a table at which seven officers sat. He wasn't there to translate. He was there to
see that glasses were filled and to fetch a bottle when
ordered. Squaw's work, his mother would have called it. It
wasn't his privilege to refuse, though he could wonder why he
was chosen rather than a striker or two, those men who pol-
ished officers' boots, tended to their uniforms and acted as per-
sonal servants. Perhaps the chore was too trifling. Perhaps the
major in charge wished to belittle him for his mixed blood.
These men weren't heavy drinkers, not when making plans, not
when they would ride on the warpath tomorrow, out from Fort
Shaw.

A secret mission, a stealing out to kill Blackfeet, a surprise
attack aimed, so they said, at Mountain Chief's band, meaning
that circumstances were circumstances, and who could tell?

Who could tell about his mother and father and Nocansee and old Heavy Runner?

A secret mission, just planned, and the fact leaked out slowly while the men were held within the fort grounds and threatened with court-martial if they revealed it.

He poured more whiskey into glasses.

Even so, he had tried. He had tried to sneak a horse from the stables and ride out to give warning. But four men guarded the horses and gates, and one of them asked, "What you doin' here, Lije?"

"Just looking. Thinking my horse needed exercise."

"Fat chance. Wait for a chinook. A horse gets out of the stables, and it's my ass."

"I was just thinking."

"Sure. Wisht I was in your place and could go in and get warm."

They had a big map on the table, their heads cocked to see it by the light of an oil lamp. The head man — Major Baker, sir, was his name — traced lines on the map and made crosses, meaning stopping places, Lije reckoned. The major had a long, bearded face and sloping shoulders and, it seemed like, the hint of the killer in his eyes.

Brother Potter would have prayed for him, but Brother Potter was dead, buried near a mining camp over west, which he was going to visit when he fell from his horse, the life gone out of him before he hit ground. Brother Potter would have prayed, but prayer wouldn't reach this man. A bullet from a Hawken would.

The lamp on the table flickered to the officers' breaths. There was another lamp in the room. Together they barely held off the dark. Shadows played on the floor when the officers moved.

The major lifted his eyes from the map. "The Blackfeet have played with us, making promises they never intended to keep. This time we show them that we mean business. No prisoners, is that understood?"

"Women and children?" one of the men asked.

"A few will be killed. That's inevitable. The rest we turn loose after burning the lodges. Tell your men no mercy."

The officers nodded.

A bullet, a war club, Lije thought, or a knife to lift the major's scalp with. His kind of mercy turned on him.

Major Baker was going on. "No matter how well we know the plans, no matter how many times we've studied them, it never hurts to review." He took a sip of whiskey. "I swear this is the last time, so bear with me, gentlemen."

All the men wore trim, dark blue coats with brass buttons, and most of them, Lije knew or guessed, were captains. Maybe one or two were lieutenants. He hadn't learned or tried to learn all the signs that showed rank. It was enough to know an officer when he saw one and to remember to "sir" him.

The major took another sip of whiskey and said, "I hope there's no risk in riding during daylight tomorrow." He looked around for agreement. "After that we go by night. By nightfall tomorrow we should be at Priest's Butte. We must allow time for the men to dismount and warm up, but still." He turned to Lije. "Why Priest's Butte, do you know?"

Lije said, making himself be polite, "The Catholic priests tried to have a mission on the Teton close to the butte. It didn't last. That was long ago. I know from my father."

"He ought to know. Will we have clear going?"

"Nothing in the way. Two lakes off the trail, one small, one shallow, frozen over now, I think."

He had spoken the truth but not been of help. They would find the way just as easily if he'd kept silent.

The major said to the officers, "We'll have our own guides, of course, but I doubt anyone knows that Teton country better than Many Tongues here. He's lived most of his life there, where I understand his father took up with a Blackfoot squaw."

"Not so," Lije broke in, not caring what happened. "My mother is his wife. They are married for many years by a Christian preacher."

"Sir."

"All right. Sir."

"So be it. Now just answer my questions. Do you know where Muddy Creek enters the Teton?"

"Yes, sir."

"How is it from Priest's Butte to that junction?"

"Some of the country is a little rough. That's all."

"Go on, on to the Marias."

"I have never been there."

"Sir."

"Sir."

"You don't know where the villages are? The camps of Mountain Chief, Big Horn, Red Horn, Big Leg, Gray Eyes?"

Major Baker's eyes went from Lije to the officers. "It doesn't matter too much. We'll find them and strike them hard according to orders. Two hundred and eighty-seven men strong, or close to it, counting those with the wagon train."

The eyes came back to Lije. "How long, how far to the Marias?"

"Three sleeps, four, depending."

"I plan to attack at dawn on the twenty-third," Major Baker told the officers. "If the weather is our enemy, it is also our friend. Think of that other enemy, the Blackfeet, all huddled in camp against the cold." He rubbed his hands. "Sitting ducks."

He turned again to Lije. "You better be right, saying you don't know where the villages are."

"Camps move where game is, where wood is, where grounds are clean," Lije answered. "My father is with Heavy Runner. Heavy Runner keeps the peace. He is friendly. He has a friendship paper."

"Just answer my questions, will you? I know that General Sully puts some trust in Heavy Runner." He spoke as if he didn't himself or didn't care. "All the same, he's a Blackfoot."

A man could stand so much and no more. Fire in the head made him speak. "Just as you are a fucking fool officer."

For just a second Major Baker sat still while the blood climbed through his beard to his forehead. Then he was on his feet. So were the others.

"Captain Ball," Major Baker said through his teeth. "I want this man thrown in the guardhouse."

"Yes, sir."

Captain Ball went to the door and called out. A sergeant came in. Captain Ball said, "Put this man in the guardhouse and keep him there."

"For how long, sir?"

Major Baker said, "Forever."

Lije told him, "I'll see you in hell."

As he was led out, Major Baker was saying, "Sorry, gentlemen. Ten o'clock in the morning then. Show the colors but only at first."

Sure. Show the colors. Then sneak, then kill, then show the colors again.

◆ ◆ ◆

With a candle to light the way, a guard unlocked a door, showed him through and led him to an empty cot. "Blankets enough to keep you warm, maybe," the guard said. "Sweet dreams."

He could hear other men in the room, breathing deep, stirring, snoring. One of them let a long fart. They were in for nothing much — for fighting, for being absent without leave, for getting drunk, for not being respectful.

Think happy, Lije told himself. Think happy if you can. Better to think back at what was than ahead at what might be.

I pray thee, O Lord . . .

Brother Potter lay dead, and there was no shovel to dig a grave with. Older Indians would have lashed the body to a stout tree branch and left him to the storms and the winds and the birds. Lije rode into the mining camp and hired a helper who had two shovels. At four feet the man said, "That's enough." It would be with the stones Lije would lay on the sod.

The man rubbed his hands. "You been through his pockets?"

"Nobody touches them. Nobody."

"All right. All right. But maybe he carried the names of relatives, like brothers and sisters."

"The whole world was his brothers and sisters."

The man looked at him queerly and said, "That's a pile of kinfolks. Time to lower him, then?"

Lije took Brother Potter's shoulders and his helper the feet. "Hefty old devil, ain't he?" the man said.

Lije let himself down into the grave, careful not to step on the body, taking with him a piece of canvas and Brother Potter's Bible and hymn book. He laid the canvas over the old face and placed the books over his heart. They put the sod over Brother Potter, and the helper rode away, taking with him some gold dust that Lije had carried ever since he left home.

Keep them safe, O Lord, I pray in Thy name.

He stood there and recited the Twenty-third Psalm, Brother Potter's favorite, and then the Lord's Prayer. Afterward he prayed to gods he didn't know, to the great god of sun and moon and stream and earth and life. He led Brother Potter's old saddle horse close to the grave. The Indians could be right. Maybe a man needed a horse, a ghost horse, in the great and everlasting hunting grounds. He shot the horse between the eyes. Then, being alone, he sat down and cried.

Guard them and keep them, Lord, my God.

Brother Potter would have prayed for their souls, not so much for their lives. They had traveled far, he and the old man, to places east and west of the mountains, to towns and beginning settlements, to mining camps and humble homes where sometimes a few of the faithful gathered, and to everybody Brother Potter preached his kind and forgiving religion. He never took up a collection, or needed to. He accepted only a bit of the offerings, saying, "Build a church. Build a house of God."

At night, or whenever time allowed, he taught Lije, using

the Bible and hymnal, and simple reading books and arithmetics that he begged or bought along the way. Teaching must be hard work, but never once had Brother Potter raised his voice except to sing the praises of Jesus.

Lord, let the major see the light, I pray thee.

Brother Potter was saying as he gave him a letter, "I have taught you all I can, son and brother. Soon it is time that you leave me. Take this letter to my friend, General De Trobriand at Fort Shaw. He is or was the commanding officer of the district of Montana. If he is not there, give it to the man in command."

So he came to Fort Shaw on the Sun or Medicine River and, after only a few questions, was taken on as interpreter.

Fort Shaw was pleasant in those late summer days. Trees shaded some of the buildings and walkways, and the wives of the officers, the few of them that were there, went strolling in the soft afternoons, and the troopers tried not to let hunger show in their faces. A man, taking a walk, might laze by the officers' quarters, the barracks, the bakery, the storehouse, the carpenter shop, the stables and granary. There was a building for the post trader, and there was a sawmill. Except for the presence of uniforms, a man could hardly believe that this little settlement, without blockhouses or loopholes, was a fort. He might think that peace had arrived.

I will lift up mine eyes unto the hills, from whence cometh my help.

The night crawled on, the long night of winter when the sun went to bed early and got up late. A bugle sounded, and a guard came in to say, "Get up, you bedbugs. Breakfast's comin', late on account all the troops had to be fed."

One by one the men rose, groaning and stretching, and filed though the door that another guard watched.

In the gray of the morning Lije stayed in his bunk. There was a window to look through when things got started.

By and by, hearing sounds, he went to the window. Watchers

had ranked themselves in front of the fort. Beyond them were the cavalrymen and the horses and the clouds of their breathing. And farther beyond, the dead land stretched in frozen ridges and flats with nothing more showing than skyline.

Major Baker, bulky in his buffalo coat, gave the order to mount. The fort band played, drums thumping and rolling and settling to the voices of horns.

The expedition rode off to the brave music, and a breeze fluttered the colors above the mounted men whose furs and blankets and robes dwarfed the horses.

There was room for a hand, a clenched hand, between the bars on the window. He drove his fist through the glass.

39

IT WAS WARM in Heavy Runner's lodge, warm when compared with the weather outside. With his capote on Summers felt comfortable. A lively fire burned. Heavy Runner's two wives sat cross-legged over at the side while the men smoked.

Night was a good time to sit by the fire and speak what came to mind. Every hour in this weather was a good time to stay inside until hunger drove a man out, hoping for game.

Summers puffed and gazed around the lodge, not for any real reason. It was the biggest lodge in the village, fitting for a chief, and by day a man could see a fading picture of the great white bear painted on the outside.

"It is a time of great hunger," Heavy Runner said.

"You speak what I know."

"The young ones dig for wild rats, and skunk, it is eaten, too."

"So I noticed."

"Not one dog is left."

Summers let him go on. Indians liked to recite, no matter if they said what everyone knew. By and by he would come around to what he really wanted to talk about. It had been so now for four or five nights, with Heavy Runner asking Summers to sit with him while he worked his way around to his subject.

"Our young men, the good ones, hunt for the buffalo and do not find him. Where are the buffalo, Bear Maker?"

"Gone south or killed off, my friend."

"We are a camp of old men and squaws and little ones, and there is much sickness. Soon, maybe, we have to eat horses." Heavy Runner made a sound in his throat. "So what is here for anyone?"

With the main point reached, Summers said as he had said before, "Those who killed Malcolm Clarke have not been turned over, and no stolen horses."

"My people did not kill him."

"Horses?"

"A few in our herd. I do not know how many. But stealing horses, it is a game with us. It has always been so."

"The white man thinks different."

"How long since the white chiefs talked to us?"

"You mark the suns and you know."

"Maybe I forget. How many?"

"Twenty-two suns by my count."

"It is so. And how long did they give us?"

"Fourteen. You know it."

"So now it is seven and one suns more than the day they say war."

"Right. Eight suns late in giving over killers and horses."

"I think they not come. War, it is foolish talk."

"It takes time to fix up a war party."

"Maybe so. But they will not fight us, Bear Maker. They trust us. I have the friendship paper."

"I hope so."

"You do not believe?"

"I do not know. I have seen things go wrong before, friends killing friends."

Heavy Runner looked into distance, as if he too had seen mix-ups. "That is truth, but I do not think so this time."

Summers rose, favoring his leg. "We will talk again, my brother."

The air grasped at his lungs when he stepped outside. A skim of snow, fallen during the day, cried underfoot. The northern lights rose and fell and rose and wavered through the frost of his breath. What did coyotes cry for?

Teal Eye was waiting for him, sitting by the side of the fire. Nocansee had his face turned toward it as if he could see.

"What does Heavy Runner say?" Teal Eye asked.

"Nothing new."

"Every night he wants to talk to you, and every day nothing happens."

"He is afraid and wants not to be. He thinks he sees soldiers coming, then tells himself no."

"He is an old woman. He could move camp across the Medicine Line."

"No use, it is said. It is agreed the soldiers could cross the line. General Sully said so."

"What do you think? Tell me," Teal Eye asked.

"Not to worry. If soldiers come, I reckon they won't bother us."

"You speak soft for me."

"Now. Now. You asked, and I told you."

Nocansee said, "I feel things wrong."

"A good rest, and you'll feel different. Let's all get to bed."

He went to sleep thinking of good buffalo meat and happy camps and old days on the beavered streams.

A shout woke him up, the end of a shout. It sounded like "Wrong camp."

He scrambled to the flap of the tepee and looked out into the gray dawn. Heavy Runner was trotting out there, waving his friendship paper. He jerked to a halt and turned and fell as a shot sounded. His paper fluttered away.

Figures sprouted up along the high rim of the river. Fire flashed along it, and powder smoke puffed up to the crack of rifles. Voices cried out in the tepees, voices of alarm, fear and pain. A child screamed. A bullet tore a hole in Summers' lodge.

"Down!" he shouted. "Down, both of you!"

He crawled back. At the rear of the tepee he strained to lift up the hide. "Get out, Teal Eye."

She didn't move. He saw eyes wide with fear, not for herself.

"Out through this hole. Quick!" He pushed at her.

She said, "But you?"

"I'm white. You love me, you go."

"Nocansee?"

"Goddamnit, go, woman! Stick to the river bank. Stick to the brush. Take the horse. Find Lije."

Nocansee said, "My mother, please go."

Summers threw a blanket over her shoulders, then another. He pushed her through the hole. Above all the noise he heard the faint rustle of her clothing against the brush. Summers saw that his rifle was loaded and hid it under the robe that he sat on.

A soldier poked his head in the tepee and strained to see. "What the hell, a white man."

"Yep."

The soldier's eyes found Nocansee. "There's one that ain't."

"He's blind."

"Why waste a bullet?" The soldier reversed his carbine and swung. The butt of it crushed Nocansee's skull. He went over without a sound.

The soldier stepped back. He started to change his hold on the rifle. Summers shot him in the head just above the eyes. The soldier fell backward, half in and half out of the tepee. His carbine skittered ahead of him.

No time to reload. Christ, for a repeater. Maybe he could make it to the soldier's carbine.

A voice outside said, "Good God, one of our men dead." A head appeared.

Summers said, "He killed my blind son."

The soldier stepped in and fired. The bullet caught Summers high in the chest. It knocked him back. The second shot went in his belly.

A second soldier came in. "I got me a turncoat son of a bitch," the first one said. "Killed his own kind."

"Finish him off."

"He's dyin'. Let him die miserable, long and miserable."

They went out.

He didn't hurt, not much, not more than a man could stand. The firing had died down to a shot now and then. There was the sound of crashing and the smell of burned things, and he knew the soldiers were yanking the tepees down over the live fires and the dead bodies. Over all the sounds rose the wailing of squaws and the crying of children and the voices of soldiers proud of themselves.

One of the soldiers shouted out, "Jesus Christ, smallpox. Let's get the hell out." Pretty soon there was no sound at all except the keening of squaws and the hard pound of hooves. Roundup of the horse herd.

He said, "Well, Nocansee . . ." not looking at where Nocansee lay. The words came back to his ears in a whisper. He couldn't bring the thought to his tongue. Now the thought was gone. He said, "Well . . ." again.